FOREX TRADING

FOR BEGINNERS

[Gordon Swing]

Text Copyright © Gordon Swing

Legal & Disclaimer

The information contained in this book and its contents is not designed to replace or take the place of any form of medical or professional advice; and is not meant to replace the need for independent medical, financial, legal or other professional advice or services, as may be required. The content and information in this book has been provided for educational and entertainment purposes only.

The content and information contained in this book has been compiled from sources deemed reliable, and it is accurate to the best of the Author's knowledge, information and belief. However, the Author cannot guarantee its accuracy and validity and cannot be held liable for any errors and/or omissions. Further, changes are periodically made to this book as and when needed. Where appropriate and/or necessary, you must consult a professional (including but not limited to your doctor, attorney, financial advisor or such other professional advisor) before using any of the suggested remedies, techniques, or information in this book.

Upon using the contents and information contained in this book, you agree to hold harmless the Author from and against any damages, costs, and expenses, including any legal fees potentially resulting from the application of any of the information provided by this book. This disclaimer applies to any loss, damages or injury caused by the use and application, whether directly or indirectly, of any advice or information presented, whether for breach of contract, tort, negligence, personal injury, criminal intent, or under any other cause of action.

You agree to accept all risks of using the information presented inside this book.

You agree that by continuing to read this book, where appropriate and/or necessary, you shall consult a professional (including but not limited to your doctor, attorney, or financial advisor or such other advisor as needed) before using any of the suggested remedies, techniques, or information in this book.

TABLE OF CONTENTS

INTRODUCTION

A forex trade transaction is characterized by selling one currency and purchasing another, for instance, you can use US dollars to buy a certain number of Euros depending on the current trading value in the market. The two currencies that characterize the forex trade are referred to as a currency pair.

Currency trading is carried out over an online platform that is referred to as the Interbank market. This market is open 24 hours each day, from Monday to Friday throughout the year. Global daily turnover in the foreign exchange currency market is in excess of US $ 5 trillion, making the currency trading market one of the biggest markets in the world in terms of value. A typical forex foreign transaction involves a situation where a buyer purchases a quantity of one currency, for example, Euros by another currency such as the US dollar. For instance, you can use US dollars to purchase Euros, similarly, you can purchase US dollars using Swiss Francs. In these trades, the exchange rate will be determined by the values of the buying currency in comparison to the currency being purchased.

CHAPTER 1:

HISTORY OF FOREX TRADING

For international trade to take place effectively, it is important for countries to have access to a market that enables them to convert local currencies to other currencies, this means that forex trading is an important factor in facilitating trade between different countries. For example, if a company in the United States was to import goods from Germany or any other European country, it can easily pay for the transaction in Euros rather than dollars by converting US dollars into euros.

History of Forex Trading

Currency exchange has always been an important part of trade throughout history. It enabled people from different regions to trade in items such as food, cloth, tools, and many other essentials. For instance, if Egyptian merchants were trading with Turkish merchants, and the Turkish merchant's currency was worth more than the Egyptian currency in terms of value, then the Turkish trader would be able to purchase more goods with fewer coins because the value of his coins would make them superior in terms of purchasing power.

Throughout history, the value of currencies has been set against commonly recognized measures such as gold or silver. Gold was typically used to fix the value of a currency by providing a measure that could equate a certain quantity of gold to a certain amount of money. Silver was also used as a measure of value for different currencies.

As early as the fifteenth century, banks had been opened to facilitate trade between different countries. The year 1880 is considered the beginning of foreign exchange and it saw the established of the gold standard. The gold standard meant that the standard economic unit of account was established based on a fixed quantity of gold. This standard was widely used in the 19th century and as well as in the early part of the 20th century.

The increase in volume called for a better trading system and this is what prompted Reuters to introduce computer monitors into the forex trading market from 1973. Hitherto the introduction of computers, telephones, and telexes were the main platforms that were used for trading quotes.

By the end of the first quarter of 2010, at least 36% of the trading volume in the forex trading market was attributed to the UK making it the largest foreign exchange trading center at the time. The United States, over the same period, accounted for at least 17% of the global foreign exchange trade while Japan was third in terms of volume with a contribution of 6% of the total traded volume.

Recent years have seen a remarkable increase in the total turnover of forex trade. By April 2010 the turnover of the options and futures market had reached the $ 166 billion mark. As it stands, over 2% of OTC turnover in foreign exchange is accounted for by forex currency derivatives.

CHAPTER 2:

WHY TO TRADE FOREX

Forex trading is also called FX or foreign exchange trading. As such, it is the art of converting one currency to another. Today, this one of the most actively traded markets with a daily trade volume of an astounding $5 trillion. Forex trading involves a network of sellers and buyers who transfer currencies to each other at agreed prices. Banks, companies, and individuals all convert currencies from one to another through this channel. Initially, foreign exchange was done mainly when people needed to travel to another country. Travelers would exchange some of their country's local currency for the foreign currency at a bank or foreign exchange broker. Today, the market has evolved, and foreign exchange is done almost purely for profit. The current type of foreign exchange is a type of investment trading. Foreign exchange trading is just like trading stocks as the traders usually speculate on the values of currencies between two currencies. Most learners usually think that forex trading is an easy venture. Contrary to popular belief, there is a high rate of failure among beginner traders of foreign exchange, and this is not as a result of any fault of their own but because there is a steep learning curve. Also, these traders may have false motives, inappropriate haste, and may be moved by unrealistic goals. It is, therefore, not surprising to find that new traders walk out empty-handed after making significant investments in the forex market

Exchange rates usually go up and down several times a minute, which means that in a day, there is a lot of action going on in the day and a business week. The currency exchange rate reflects the health of an economy. If therefore, the US economy is doing better than the Eurozone, then the dollar will go up compared to the dollar. There are some basic concepts that you have to understand if you intend to get into foreign exchange trade. They include:

Spread. Spread is the difference between the ask and bid price. The ask price is the price at which you can buy, and the bid price is the price at which you can sell. Usually, these prices are stated as forex quotes on the platforms used for trading, and they occur on each currency pair.

Leverage. Leverage is the amount a forex account broker offers you for trade. For instance, if your broker offers you a 200:1 leverage, then it means that they are allowing you to trade with 200 times more money than you have deposited. Just as is the case with stocks, with leverage you can buy 200 more times than what you have, but you have to be prepared for any eventualities, which are 200 times bigger profits or 200 times losses. Before placing a trade, it is important to understand and evaluate whether you need leverage.

Major banks top the system, and they put in big orders compared to the rest, that is why they stay on top. Major banks also move or influence the market. Banks communicate among themselves through the electronic brokering services. Next on the ladder is the retail market makers and ECNs and brokers.

Lastly, there are retail traders at the bottom and who do not have any influence on the market.

Forex trading has its advantages and disadvantages. It is important that you know about them, so that you will know what to expect once you start trading foreign currencies. Let us examine them one by one:

Advantages of Trading Forex

Fun

Trading currencies is fun to do. In fact, it is very easy to get addicted to it. It is like a game that adults can truly enjoy, especially if you are making positive profits. It is fun to look at charts and choose the currency pair that you want to invest in. Developing a strategy and making your own market predictions can be fun. Overall, the whole activity of being a forex trader can be a truly fun experience.

Demo account

Most forex traders will allow you to preview their services by providing you with a demo account. A demo account will allow you not only to test your broker's trading platform, but it will also allow you to trade in a real-market environment. A demo account can also be used to test your strategy. As a forex broker, testing your strategy before using it with real money is an important habit that you definitely have to do.

More choices

With around 28 major currency pairs to choose from, you will never run out of currency pairs to trade. This ensures that you will not find a moment to sit idly. Also, considering the nature of forex, you are sure that there is always a currency pair among the chances that will make profits.

Convenient

Forex trading is convenient to do. All you need is to connect to the Internet and you can start trading using the trading platform that is provided by your broker. You can easily open and close positions with just a few clicks of a mouse.

Easy to enter

It is easy to enter the forex market. You can start participating in the market simply by going online. You can make trades in the comfort of your home. You also do not need a high capital. There are many online brokers that will allow you to trade even with a small investment.

Fair market

There is no authority that controls or unduly influences the forex market. Of course, certain things and event may affect the price of currencies, but they cannot continuously do so for an extended period of time. The forex market is very big with lots of different participants.

24-hour market

The forex market is open round-the-clock. Hence, you can

trade in the morning, in the afternoon, in the evening, or evening at 2am or 3am. It is up to you to decide when you want to participate in the market. Although the forex market follows a schedule, once it opens for the week, you can rest assured that it will remain open round the clock until it closes by the end of the week.

High liquidity

The FX market is famous for having high liquidity. Therefore, you can expect to be able to buy and sell currencies easily since there is always someone who will take the other side of your trade. You can never get "stuck" and there is definitely no waiting time for buying and selling currencies. It is a very active market.

Low cost

The main cost in forex trading is normally included already in the spread. Therefore, you no longer need to worry about any exchange or clearing fee, and not even a brokerage fee. Under normal market conditions, the retail transaction cost is even lower than 0.1%. If you are working with a large dealer, then it is normally lower than 0.7%. Of course, this may increase depending on your leverage. Since you no longer have to worry about so many costs that you need to cover, you can put all your focus on what really matters, and that is making a profit.

Leverage

It is not a secret that many people like forex trading because it will allow you to leverage. As we have discussed in the previous chapter, leveraging will allow you to invest a small amount of money but trade using a substantial capital. Needless to say, this will allow you to rake in more profits. Many traders do not have enough money to start up with a decent capital. Leveraging will allow you to spend and risk less and at the same time have a high-profit return.

High-profit potential

Forex trading has a high-profit potential. In fact, there are professional FX traders who have quit their day job and trade currencies for a living. Some people have also attained financial freedom by forex trading. Trading currencies has long been established as something that can be very lucrative. Of course, you also need to spend time and efforts in order to make it worthwhile and profitable. When you engage in FX trading, even a small investment of $100 can grow by more than 300% in just a short period of time. Compare this with investing in stocks where a profit of 20% in a year is already considered high. Indeed, if you have money that you can use to invest, learning forex trading is most probably the best thing that you can do that can lead you to financial freedom.

Disadvantages of Trading Forex

Hard to predict

There are multiple factors that affect the forex market. In fact, this is the reason why forex traders usually rely on technical analysis. With so many factors that influence the prices of the different currencies, it becomes almost impossible to predict the price movement of a currency. Of course, you can always apply an effective strategy, but it does not change the fact that the forex market is hard, if not impossible, to predict.

If you were to consider all the elements that can influence the outcome of a particular trade, then you will have to spend lots of hours just to be able to analyze everything. However, the forex market is a continuously moving market. Therefore, by the time that you finish analyzing a set of data, there will definitely be a new set of information that you could look into.

Self-taught

Unlike investing in stocks where you can ask for assistance from trade advisors and portfolio managers, dealing with forex is ultimately something that you do on your own. It is not a surprise for beginners to lose their initial investment. Unfortunately, after experiencing a bad loss, they usually get discouraged, which prevents them from fully learning the ins and outs of trading. Hence, when you are just starting out, it is important that you admit to yourself that you are just a newbie. As much as possible, take advantage of the demo account that is provided to you by your broker, so that you can familiarize yourself with the actual trading environment. It is also advised that you start out small even if you have a big amount of money that ready for trading in your account.

Less regulated

Since forex trading is not regulated by any central authority, traders usually rely on their broker to facilitate a trade. If you get lucky and end up working with an unreliable broker, you will only get scammed and cheated in the process. Also, since you will be relying on the assistance extended to you by a broker, you may not have total control over your trades and orders. Therefore, in order to prevent this from happening, it is important that you only work with regulated and legitimate brokers. Since forex takes place in an over-the-counter market, you need to be careful in choosing your broker.

Volatility

The prices of different currencies are affected by many factors. The forex market can, from time to time, be highly volatile. You can also expect for some unforeseeable events to take place. The bad part is that traders may not be able to do anything about them when they occur. For example, during the time when Iceland got bankrupt, forex traders holding Icelandic krona could not do anything but watch how they were holding a something that has significantly depreciated. This is unlike in investing in stocks where shareholders can somehow pressure the board of directors to act more promptly and take appropriate actions. To avoid being a victim of the high volatility of the market, it is well advised that you limit your losses and always be sure to use a well-planned approach when trading.

Lower return

It is true that you can make lots of money with forex even if you just invest a small amount since you can use the power leverage. It is also true that trading currencies has a higher profit potential than just investing in stocks. However, forex trading is not the one that offers the highest payout. Of you want a higher return, then you might want to consider options trading instead of forex trading. With options trading, you can get as high as 90% return for every trade that lasts as fast as two minutes, or even less. However, it is worth noting that options trading is so much riskier than forex trading. Options trading is like gambling in the casino. There is also no way to leverage your position.

Risky

Although people who engage in forex trading are in it for the profit that they can make, the unfortunate truth is that many of these traders end up losing their investment. It is risky to participate in forex, especially if you do not know what you are doing. In fact, if you do not have knowledge of forex and simply jump in without preparation, it is most likely that you will suffer a big loss in just a few days. If you get too careless, then you can expect to lose your money on the very first day of trading. Even those who have been trading for years are still careful before they open a position. As a beginner, you need to be more cautious of your actions.

Although you are well encouraged to do all the necessary

research and analysis before making any trade, there is no amount of preparation that can guarantee 100% it will give you a favorable outcome. Literally every trade that you make has its risks.

CHAPTER 3:

FOREX MARKET OPEN
AND CLOSE TIME

Anyone can trade in Forex as long as you have the starting capital and some knowledge about forex markets. Also, if you don't have enough capital, big financial organizations lend small and medium-sized traders money to use in the forex market. However, you must prove that you are knowledgeable in forex trading.

Forex exchange has been around for very many years, and some say that it is as old as the invention of national currencies. Over the years, the market has grown so much so that it is the biggest market across the world. However, it has not been accessible to the public as easily as it is today. From the 1990s when the era of the internet begun, many retail forex brokers have established routes through which anyone can trade in currencies so long as they can access the internet and have some money. There is a lot of hype and information about forex trade on the internet, but not everybody understands how to select and open an account.

Currently, opening a forex account has become as easy as opening a bank account or another type of brokerage account. Some of the typical requirements are a name, phone number, address, email, a password, account currency type, country of citizenship, date of birth, employment status, and tax ID or

Social security number. Opening an account may also require one to answer some financial questions such as their net worth, annual income, trading objectives, and trading experience. Before one starts to trade on the foreign exchange market, they should make some considerations to ensure that they have a positive, secure and successful experience.

The right broker

The first step to trading well is to find the right broker. The activities of forex exchange are decentralized, and there are hardly any regulations. Because of the over the counter nature, traders are advised to identify a reliable broker. This involves conducting researches on the reputation of the broker; to identify if there is a history of irregular practices. One may also want to comprehensively understand the services offered by the particular broker before setting up an account. While some brokerages support basic and plain vanilla activities, others offer very sophisticated trading platforms. Some brokers will offer the trader analytical resources to support better decision making while others won't.

Again, a trader should assess the fees and commissions for different brokers. The majority of Brokers charge some fees for their services through the bid-ask spread and, in many cases, it is not a large percentage. However, some brokerages have some other fees and commissions, and they might be hidden from the trader. When one is considering the extra costs, he/she should check if it is worthwhile.

The procedure

Opening a foreign exchange account is not hard, but traders should have a few things in order to get started. The trader will have to provide some identification information such as name, phone number, country of origin et cetera. Besides, the trader will be required to state his/her trade intentions and their level of knowledge and experience in the trade. The steps of opening an account may vary depending on the brokerage firm, but normally it involves:

Accessing the website of the broker and study the accounts available. The accounts include small ones where the trader can trade with minimum capital such as mini accounts or the sophisticated accounts designed for experienced traders such as standard trading account.

Completing an application form,

Getting registered (user name and password) in order to access the account.

Log in to the client portal and arrange for a transfer of money from the bank to the forex account. These deposits can be made through credit or debit card, checks, or electronic transfers.

Once the funds are transferred, the trader is ready to start trading. Before trading, the trader may review the recommendations made by the brokers or extra services offered such as simulator programs.

The use of margins

Once a trader has opened an account, he/she has to decide whether to apply a margin or not. A margin is a leverage move whereby the broker offers the trader a loan in order to increase the available capital. A broker can offer a margin on capital for any rate between 50:1 and 400:1 depending on the country they operate from. The amount that a trader wants in terms of margin will determine the amount of capital that he/she will deposit in the account. The deposit acts as collateral for the trading activities. True, margins increase potential profits, but one should be warned that they also increase the risks. In case of loss, the trader will be required to cover the costs even if they are beyond the initial investment.

If you are a savvy trader then there is already plenty of money to be made trading in the forex, or the foreign exchange currency market, however, if you take this type of trading into the day trading arena then the potential for profit ratchets up even further, as does the potential for great personal financial risk. If you have not traded in the forex market before then it is important to start off small and work your way up to larger trades, just until you know what its unique intricacies have in store for you. Just because you have a strategy that you know has the potential to work, doesn't mean that it will work regardless of whether or not you implement it properly, follow the rules and you will have a greater chance of doing both.

Always start with the right pairs: As a new forex day trader, you will likely find success when it comes to trading in the

EUR/USD and GBP/USD pairs most readily, simply because they will be the ones that it will the easiest to find relevant data on with the least amount of work or when you are working up against a strict deadline, the strategy outlined below will work with any pairs you choose, however, so it is really up to you.

Begin each day the right way: While you might find it helpful to trade during the earliest part of the day, you really only need about 2 hours per day to implement this strategy assuming all goes according to plan. You can choose any period when the UK section of the market is open and going strong, it doesn't need to be at any set point in time. Once you have established the direction that the market is heading for the day you will want to trade into any trends that you find and then wait for the pullback to occur. This will likely happen somewhere near the trendline which means it is likely to be at a point just above a previous major swing low. After the pullback, has occurred you will need to wait until the price stabilizes for at least two minutes prior to moving forward.

Forex strategies

Short-term forex strategy: If you are interested in trading in the forex market in the short term then it is important to keep in mind that your goal should always be to control the amount of risk you take on as much as possible. This will make it easier for you to deal in charts that tend to offer shorter time frames than many forex traders deal in. This doesn't mean that you are going to want to stick to the short-term charts exclusively, however, as this can cause your profits to be lower overall than they would otherwise be.

To trade effectively in the short-term, the first thing you are going to want to be on the lookout for is a pair of moving averages on the hourly charts. The trading platform that you use should be able to automatically generate what you are looking for based on the timeframe that you choose. After you have the indicators that you are looking for, you will then be able to more easily utilize them as a sort of guidepost that will make it easier to determine how the market is moving in the timeframe in question so that you will be able to look before you leap as it were. If the resulting short moving average is less than the larger moving average then you will want to take a long position, otherwise, you will want to take a short position instead.

Once you have determined the trend that you are looking for, the next thing you will need to do is to look at the entries that are going to match the direction of the trend you are following. The goal here should be to successfully locate the momentum that you saw on the longer chart in either the 15-minute or 5-minute chart that you will actually want to do work in.

When utilizing this strategy, it is important to remember that the timing is not always going to be right when it comes to buying in. Rather, you will want to be patient and wait for a profitable position to come along. The best way to do so is to look for what is known as the exponential moving average.

When looking for this type of average you are going to need to find a trigger that is known as an 8-period exponential on the 5-minute chart. When this exponential begins to move in the direction of the overall trend you will know that it will soon pick up speed and increase in such a way that will generate a profit.

While this strategy does take a fair degree of micromanaging, it is beneficial in several ways. The first is that waiting until you see the right trigger means that other traders who are working in the short-term are always going to be creating action based on the pair you are looking to trade leading to more reliable profits. Furthermore, this strategy is a great way for those whose starter capital might not be where they want it to be as it will allow the savvy trader to jump on specific currency pairs before the serious momentum starts and the bullish nature of the pair pushes the price beyond their means.

On the other hand, this strategy will also allow those who utilize it to sell various currencies for the greatest amount of value possible because it lets them get out early. If a price experiences a short-term retracement, however, then the price is going to swing and you will need to be able to determine what you are seeing in order to prevent yourself from making a mistake.

In order to maximize your profits in this scenario, you will need to set up your stop losses at a point that is just below the currency's last high water mark. Alternatively, if you are invested in short positions then you will want to set your stop losses so that they are just above the current low point to prevent a loss. This makes the short-term strategy extremely versatile as long as you are able to keep your emotions in check and set the right stops.

Forex hedging: A good rule of thumb is the longer the term of any put options you use, and the lower the strike price, the more reliable the hedging strategy is going to be. While the initial cost is going to be significantly higher than not using a hedging strategy, the longer it stays in place the more cost effective it becomes. This makes it a particularly effective go-to when you are considering long term strategies. It is also much more cost effective to hedge indices as opposed to individual currency pairs.

You will also want to be aware that hedging will mitigate risk related to a dramatic change in value, but is ineffective when it comes to countering the risk that comes from general underperformance, something that will only be clear in the long term. This means it is really only worthwhile for risky trades that promise large payoffs. Additionally, you will need to keep in mind that not all forex brokers allow hedging so it is worth looking into before you mentally commit to anything.

An excellent way to maximize the value of a hedge is to make a point of always choosing the put option with the greatest amount of available lead time. This is simply a matter of cost/benefit analysis as one option that lasts for six months is going to be much less expensive than two three month options. The ultimate marginal cost of maximizing your option provides you with the least expensive form of daily trade protection possible.

This is useful as you can turn a six-month option into a twelve-month option while still keeping the same strike price. This is known as rolling and it will let you take advantage of market changes as they appear. Assuming you have a strike price that is below the average market value you can keep an option rolling for years with only a minimal extra cost. This is exceptionally useful if you combine it with a highly leveraged investment that promises a large return as it mitigates a large amount of the potential risk.

Rolling a put forward can also allow you to know you have a relatively cheap hedge into play when you need it. A calendar is created when a long term and short term option are bought and sold respectively using the same strike price to start the trade. The end goal here is ideally to allow the shorter put to expire harmlessly after its maximum and allowing the long put to then serve as a future hedge moving forward. While a properly implemented calendar spread can create an extremely cheap and effective hedge that can be used essentially indefinitely, without the proper research you can be exposing yourself to significant additional risk. Consider the extreme long term before attempting to utilize this particular strategy.

CHAPTER 4 :

ESSENTIAL TERMINOLOGIES FOR FOREX TRADING BEGINNERS

As with most specialized areas, the Forex market comes with its own terminology that can be utterly undecipherable to the uninitiated. Before we discuss how to trade in Forex, let's get you acquainted with those words and phrases to help you navigate the information more easily.

Ask Price: This is the price that a seller is willing to accept for a trade on the market.

Spread: This is the difference between the bid and ask price and is where the broker makes their money. The more volatility in the market, the wider the spread is likely to be.

Exchange Rate: A familiar term for vacationers, this refers to the value of one currency in terms of another. For instance, how many Euros you would get for one Australian dollar.

Currency Pairs: The Forex market does not deal with individual currencies, but with pairs of them. For example, the U.S. dollar combined with the Canadian dollar. Some are much more widely traded than others.

Cross Currency: A trade in which neither currency is the U.S. dollar.

G7 and G20: These seven countries – the United States, Italy, Japan, France, Germany, Canada and the United Kingdom – are the countries with the most major economic developments and represent over two thirds of the world's wealth. Their currencies are stable, creating currency pairings that have high volume and volatility. The G20 includes these countries but also others including China, India, Argentina, Australia, South Africa, South Korea, Mexico, Saudi Arabia, Turkey, Brazil and the European Union. These together make up four fifths of the world's trade and 85 percent of the gross domestic product on the planet. These currencies are the ones you will focus on as a trader.

Restricted Currencies: Some governments do not allow trading or speculation with their currencies. This can be because there is a limited availability, concern about the effect of speculation or a desire to control foreign investment.

Pip: This refers to the smallest possible increment by which a currency can move in price. Some currencies are quoted to four or five decimal places, so a pip refers to 0.0001 or 0.00001 of that pound, franc or Euro. Others are quoted only to two decimal places, so a pip is 0.01.

Volume: In Forex trading, this refers to the number of units being traded at one time. One currency may only have five or ten transactions taking place on it over the course of a day, while another may have thousands upon thousands. The former therefore has a low volume of trade, while the latter has a high volume.

Volatility: This refers simply to how much change there is in the trading price of a currency over time. The most that price changes, the more volatile that currency is said to be.

Margin: If you don't have enough money to invest in a trade, you can get a secured loan from your broker to increase your capital. This is known as using margin. Doing so involves a great deal of risk as, if the trade is not successful, you will find yourself in significant debt.

Margin call: This term refers to your broker requiring you to settle your account, usually when a trade reaches a certain level of risk.

CHAPTER 5:

STEPS TO SUCCESSFULLY TRADING FOREX

Step 1: Begin By Defining Your Goals

Before starting your journey as a Forex trader, it is important to have a clear idea about what you would like to achieve and how you intend to get to this destination. Ensure that you have clearly drawn your goals and mastered them in mind. After defining your goals, try to assess through the different trading methods available. Select the best method that fits you and ensures that this trading method will enable you to achieve your set goals. This is because each trading method has its own risk profile which will require you as a trader to develop some attitude as well as approach so as to be a successful Forex trader. For instance, if you are this type of person whose instincts does not allow to go to sleep when there is an open market position, clearly you are best fit for day trading. However, if you are this type of a person who is ready to take time and wait for some periods for trade to appreciate, then you are the best fit to be a position trader. It is appropriate that you be sure of your personality. Your personality must fit your trading style. Forex trading at times is stressful thus be sure that your personality matches the method of trade you have chosen.

Step 2: Trade with the right mindset

If you ever hope to stick around the market long enough to think of yourself as an expert trader, there are several skills you are going to need to become very adept at using. First and foremost, this means always trading with a cool head, no matter what. When you are trading, your goal should be to be as emotionless and robotic as possible. The only thing that matters when you are trading is the numbers and if you worry about anything else while doing so, you are doing it wrong. Trading in the forex market successfully often means having the ability to make split second decisions, something that just can't be done if you let your emotions get in the way. Understanding the fact that your emotions are only getting in the way and acting on that fact are two extremely different things. The first emotion that you are going to need to focus on banishing is anger. It can be easy to get angry when a trade that appears as though it is going to be a sure thing suddenly turns sideways,but a more effective use of that time is to instead immediately do what is required to minimize the losses, rather than standing there yelling at them. Aside from anger, the most common emotion that you are likely to come across is going to be fear. It can be easy to become afraid, especially if you broke the 2 percent rule and invested too heavily in a single pair; that doesn't mean it is productive, however, and indeed it can be even more dangerous than anger as it can be paralyzing as well. To prevent this from happening you will need to train yourself to push the emotion aside and act on the facts if you ever hope to find real success in the forex market.

Step 3: Be clear on the right approach for you:

When you first start trading in forex it is important to have a clear idea of what your general aversion to risk is as well as how you handle your emotions when it matters most. You then want to choose time frames and strategies that align with your natural inclinations rather than changing your personal comfort level to suit a plan that someone else claims worked for them.

To start, you are going to want to consider the time frame you are primarily working in and make sure that it aligns with your temperament. If you are looking for lower risk, then short time frames are a good choice, otherwise, if you are instead looking to spend less time staring at a computer screen something longer is probably the right choice.

Step 4: Keep the risk in mind:

Before you go ahead and make the decision to ultimately pull the trigger on any potential currency trade you are currently considering, the first thing you are going to want to go ahead and make sure that you know how likely you are to get your money back as well as actually turn a profit. This is why it is always so important to analyze the data that you gather as there is no other way of determining the mood the market is in which means essentially going into a trade just to gamble, and there are better ways to gamble than through the forex market. Additionally, you will want to know when to go ahead and cut your losses and having a clear idea of the overall level of risk will make this easier to determine as well.

With a clear idea of what sort of risk is going to be required for the trade in question, you will then have more tools at your disposal when it comes time to actually mitigate the risk that you have found, or at least to decrease it as much as possible. Ensuring that the odds of actually turning a profit are in your favor means setting a tight stop loss and not letting your emotions get in the way in the heat of the moment. The point that you start a trade and the point that you set your stop loss at can be considered the maximum amount of risk you are accepting for a given trade.

It is important to always determine the acceptable amount of risk you can handle before you actually make the trade when your emotions are of a nominal concern. If you wait to set a stop loss until after the trade is already in progress, then you run the risk of letting your emotions cloud your better judgement and losing profits in the process.If you feel the need to change your stop loss coming on then you are going to want to take a moment and consider exactly what it is you are thinking about doing and if it is something that you would consider if you were just getting in at that moment. With a few moment's consideration, your answer should be clear.

This means that if you start off with $ 5,000 of available funds to spend in the forex market you are never going to want to invest more than $ 100 on a specific currency pair. While this amount may seem limiting when you are on a roll and your trades are proceeding successfully, it will actually serve to keep you trading successfully in the long run as it will ensure that you are never completely wiped out after just one or two trades. Rather, you would need to make 50 bad trades in a row in order for your trading capital to be used up completely, something that is unlikely for even the most novice forex trader.

Being successful in the forex market is all about long term wins outshining short term losses. Any trading plan can be successful as long as it leads to a profit slightly more than 50 percent of the time. While these payouts won't be anything to write home about, you are guaranteed to keep moving in the right direction as long as you take it slow. If your available trade capital is relatively modest you are going to want to stick to mini lots until you build up a larger amount of capital to invest with. Mini lots will allow you to risk as much as a 50-pip margin without exceeding 2 percent of $ 5,000.

Step 5: Never panic:

When a trader panics, he sees nothing but losses in the market with no way of ending the session by turning the tables and making it a lucrative trade or a less disastrous one. In the forex market, when a trader loses a large sum of money, another trader is possibly earning large profits. This simple equation is enough at least to help traders to be much more practical in response to panic levels in the forex market. However, observation and experience have shown us anything, but.

There are many things that can cause traders in the forex market to panic such as market volatility, price fluctuations and so on. A frightful trader will definitely make different kinds of disastrous errors from closing positions too early to performing away from his logical analysis and be driven by illusions and emotions. All in all, the panicky trader can barely contain his demeanor,thus intensifying the damage.

When trading in the forex market, traders must learn to not let their emotions influence their trading decisions. Minimizing the role of emotions is the key to understand how to manage the crisis.

Leverage is always the control of the forex account owner, therefore, she can set it at any value, but bearing in mind the consequences. While leverage amplifies the gains or losses of a trade, it also amplifies the emotional response of trading as well. Eventually, emotional pressures may prove to be the most dangerous and negative impact of leverage. To deal with emotional problems is to look at things at a practical and logical approach and easiest way to do that is to learn, study and understand market behavior.

Step 6: Keep the risk in mind

Before you go ahead and make the decision to ultimately pull the trigger on any potential currency trade you are currently considering, the first thing you are going to want to go ahead and make sure that you know how likely you are to get your money back as well as actually turn a profit. This is why it is always so important to analyze the data that you gather as there is no other way of determining the mood the market is in which means essentially going into a trade just to gamble, and there are better ways to gamble than through the forex market. Additionally, you will want to know when to go ahead and cut your losses and having a clear idea of the overall level of risk will make this easier to determine as well.

With a clear idea of what sort of risk is going to be required for the trade in question, you will then have more tools at your disposal when it comes time to actually mitigate the risk that you have found, or at least to decrease it as much as possible. Ensuring that the odds of actually turning a profit are in your favor means setting a tight stop loss and not letting your emotions get in the way in the heat of the moment. The point that you start a trade and the point that you set your stop loss at can be considered the maximum amount of risk you are accepting for a given trade.

It is important to always determine the acceptable amount of risk you can handle before you actually make the trade, when your emotions are of a nominal concern. If you wait to set a stop loss until after the trade is already in progress, then you run the risk of letting your emotions cloud your better judgement and losing profits in the process. If you feel the need to change your stop loss coming on then you are going to want to take a moment and consider exactly what it is you are thinking about doing and if it is something that you would consider if you were just getting in at that moment. With a few moment's consideration, your answer should be clear. To keep your emotions from getting the better of you, prior to going into each trade you are going to want to keep in mind the point that you will always get out when you are happy with your profits, no matter what. When it comes to maximizing your profits, a stopping point is just as important as a good stop loss point. You may be tempted to stay in as long as possible in an effort to squeeze the most profit out of a good trade as possible, but this will lose you more than it will make you in the long run, guaranteed. Instead, the right choice is to cash out half of your holdings and then pick a new point further up so that you protect your profits while also maximizing them.

Finally, regardless of how much of a sure thing a specific trade may appear to be, you need to get in the habit of never investing more than you can afford to lose in a single trade. This means that if you start with $ 5,000 that you can invest in the forex market then you never want any single trade to cost you more than $ 100. This is what is known as the 2 percent rule and it is crucial to remaining financially solvent while investing in forex, especially when you are just starting out. While you will likely come up against moments where you want nothing more than to buck this trend, especially when you are riding high on a quality pair, sticking with it is what separates successful forex traders from amateurs. If you can't afford to lose it, don't put it in the pot, it is as simple as that.

CHAPTER 6:

DIVERGENCE AND IT'S IMPORTANCE

What Is Divergence Trading?

By genuinely recognizing the title "difference," one can without an awful lot of a stretch tell that uniqueness replacing is a type exchanging mounted in disharmony or deviation. Disparity Forex exchanging methods are as frequently as feasible utilized with the aid of cash dealers around the world.

In principle, expenses and pointers have to go a similar way at equal rates. On the off danger that the value arrives at a higher high, at that factor, the marker has to arrive at a more significant high. On the off threat that the benefit comes at a decrease steep, at that factor, the pointer needs to go with the identical pattern. The equal applies to lower lows and higher lows.

In the match that the fee and the related pointers don't associate, at that point, you can tell that some progress is going to happen. The excellent markers to use in dissimilarity changing are Stochastics, RSI, MACD, and Trade Volume.

A bullish distinction occurs when the award in the marker is extra advantageous than the difference in the price — bearish disparity is a unique way. While applying this differentiation, there are four indispensable sorts of dissimilarity:

- Regular Bullish

- Hidden Bullish

- Regular Bearish

- Hidden Bearish

We will make clear every kind and how to trade the concerning disparity Forex procedure.

Regular Bullish

Standard divergences are utilized as an apparatus to exhibit inversions. This EUR/USD month to month outline demonstrates the fee of making a decrease low for two days. In any case, the energy in MACD and Stochastics didn't relate to that of the cost activity, making higher lows. This hedge a possible inversion of the sample or perchance a comply with the downtrend or something similar.

'In reverse Head and Shoulders' models are something in opposition to head and shoulders. All standards apply, anyway they are essential upside down. For this circumstance, the neck zone furthermore fills in as an obstacle. It infers we should plan to buy upon the break of the neck zone. Like head and shoulders, they may be straight, climbing, or sliding.

Regular Bearish

As we can see from the USD/CHF chart, the price reached a high in the previous week and then made a higher high the following week. On the other hand, the MACD indicator at the bottom of the chart is making lower highs. This is called 'Regular Bearish Divergence' and indicates a fall in the price to come.

In this case, since we are in an uptrend, we should expect a retracement. After entering at the top, we should look to get out of the trade at the uptrend line.

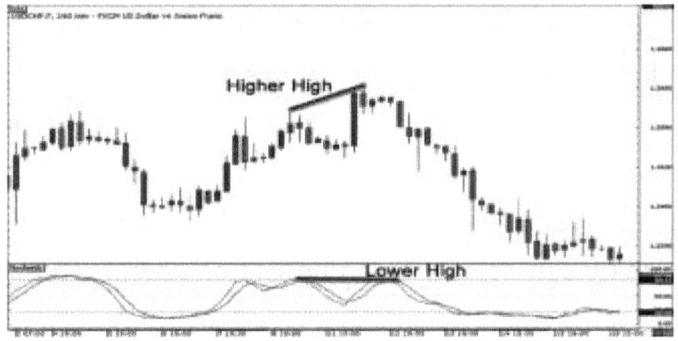

Candle Strategy in Forex

Neither one of the candlesticks examples can be an exchanging signal itself, nor would it be able to be utilized for a showing of the potential sections. The model demonstrates the desires in the market and signalizes the possible changes. For looking for the passage, another technique for examination, as opposed to candles, ought to be utilized.

If you lean toward day exchanging, being doubtful to pointers, at that point Japanese candle Forex exchanging system would live up to your desires. Candle examples empower a broker to decide the market circumstance just as organic market balance.

Characteristics of the candle design investigation

The more extended the «body» of the candle in Forex, the more grounded the Momentum and the more prominent the possibility to move in the indicated bearing. A bullish candle with the enormous body and the short shade demonstrates that the purchasers impact the market more than the dealers. A «bearish» flame with the colossal body and quick «shade» implies that the market supply is more grounded than interest. A long «shade» explicit way suggests that during the time spent the candle's arrangement in Forex; the organic market parity has moved. The progressions of the market desires can be dictated by contrasting the candles and one another.

The little shade from either side demonstrates more prominent odds of the development distinct way. Generally equivalent «shades» gave the candle's body is little (Doji candles for Forex design) speaks to advertise uncertainty - the weight on the purchaser's and dealer's cost is around the equivalent. In such conditions, even a little development in volume of exchange may cause a stable value development; all the more regularly, there is a pattern to switch.

The principle candle exchanging frameworks:

The candle designs which might be characterized as inversion examples caution about inversion pattern as well as about the parallel development start or exit from it; and now and then about decrease of the development's speed without altering of the course. Any example bodes well just where it arrives at the most grounded level. If an inversion example succeeds, at that point, it will be trailed by constant distinct development.

All exchanging examples made up of 1-2 candles would lose their importance if, during current development (pattern or revision in value development), this example applied more than once. This is particularly valid for Doji candle designs. The most dependable Japanese candle sign shows up on the Daily period. Following time allotment decline, the unwavering quality of the sign brings down.

A case of exchanging candles technique dependent on Engulfing design

Candle Forex exchanging system utilizes this candle design as an inversion signal or the revision starts.

Trading asset: It is any currency pair.

Trading period: This is the European and sessions.

Timeframe: This usually D1 or H1.

Candlestick trading strategy for a signal to buy:

The development of a candle «engulfing» example is required on the low of the descending pattern.

The sign is affirmed: it tends to be a Doji candle example or one all the more Engulfing case a similar way.

Low of the first Engulfing example must not be recharged; in addition - the more remote the value, the more grounded an exchanging signal.

Right now of the following candle opening, we will open a long position. Stop Loss will be fixed underneath a Low affirmation sign.

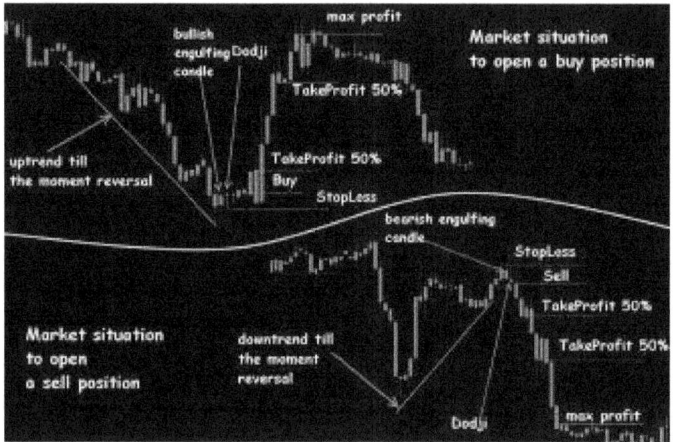

Candlestick strategy Forex for the signal to sell:

The development of the candle «engulfing» example is required on the high of the upward pattern.

The sign is affirmed: Doji candle example or one all the more Engulfing case a similar way.

High of the first Engulfing example must not be recharged.

We will open a short position right now of the following candle arrangement. Stop Loss will be set over the High affirmation signal.

The candle Forex methodology with «Free candle» pointer

The exchanging methodology utilizes candle designs with a high unwavering quality level and sliding standard for the assurance of the present pattern. EMA(9) is prompted for the famous money pair exchanging on the M15 period. «Free candle» is viewed as a full-fledged 15-minute flame, body, and shade of which don't contact the EMA (9) line, and the end cost of the candles in Forex exchanging isn't higher/bring down the past outrageous. «Free candle» must have the typical «body» and regular «shade» («hammer,» «dodgy» inversion examples, and GAP are not relevant).

I am exchanging resources: EUR/USD, USD/JPY, USD/CHF, GBP/USD, EUR/GBP, EUR/JPY, GBP/JPY.

I am exchanging period: the European and the US exchanging session. Candle Forex exchanging the times of the market's uncertainty isn't fitting.

The fundamental pattern's heading is dictated by EMA(9). For the extended position (purchase), the presence of the «free» bullish flame above EMA(9) is required. The rear light's entrance after «free candle» or a Buy Stop request ought to be somewhat higher than the end cost. The Stop Loss is fixed at the maximum level of the free candle.

And for a short position (sell), a «free bearish candle» ought to be fixed underneath the moving normal. The section at the opening of the following flame relies upon the market or ought to be made by a pending Sell Stop request. A Stop Loss ought to be fixed 3-5 beneath min of the «free light.

For the setting of Taking Profit, two scopes of the free light ought to be used.

A decent minute for the section with regards to candle system exchanging respect to first cash sets shows up inside 15-30 minutes after the European session opening when the market bearing has been resolved. The standard length of the open arrangement is as long as 60 minutes. It isn't prescribed to exchange without Stop Loss or enter inside initial 5 minutes of every hour.

The arrangement ought to be opened except if:

good ways from shutting cost of the «free candle» to EMA(9) is under 3-4;

The body of the «free candle» is under 10.

From the scientific desire planned, the «free candle» Forex candle exchanging is adequately viable, if the arrangements are not made time after time and just in dependable designs.

Ascending Triangle Pattern

This triangle example has its upper side level and the lower one climbing. As such, the highest points of this triangle are on a similar level, and the bottoms are expanding. This sort of triangle regularly has a bullish character. When you recognize this triangle on the outline, you ought to be set up to catch a bullish value move equivalent to in any event the size of the triangle. As such, breakouts through the upper level (the level side) is utilized for setting section focuses for long positions. This is a sketch of the rising triangle outline design:

The dark lines above show the value activity inside the triangle development. The blue lines allude to the sides of the triangle, which contains the value activity. The red lines relate to the size of the triangle and its potential objective, which is commonly a 1:1 estimated move. At the point when an ascending triangle is framed during a bullish pattern, we anticipate a continuation of the design.

Diving Triangle Pattern

As noted before, the climbing and slipping triangles are an equal representation of one another. In that capacity, the sliding triangle example has the contrary trademark. The flat side of the sliding triangle is underneath the value activity. The upper side of the triangle is slanted downwards. In a bearish market, the plunging triangle has a bearish potential equivalent to in any event the size of the example. Thus, the sliding triangle is utilized to open short positions after the cost has broken its lower (level) side. How about we see the sketch of the slipping triangle:

At the point when the dropping triangle is made during a bearish value propensity, we anticipate that the pattern should proceed.

It is essential to refer to that the rising and the plunging triangles some of the time get through the slanted level, causing false hedge and catching a few merchants en route. Similar remains constant at the level cost zone. You ought to consistently attempt to sit tight for the end of the flame to affirm the breakout. This will help lessen a significant number of the bogus sign.

Rising/Falling Wedge

The rising and falling wedges are like the mounting and the sliding triangle designs. Notwithstanding, the rising and the falling wedges have no flat side. The two sides of the prongs are inclining a similar way. We should portray the two sorts of wedges you will discover on the value outline.

Rising Wedge

This is a triangle diagram design, where the two sides are slanted upwards. The value makes higher tops and considerably higher bottoms. This makes the two rising lines collaborate, creating a kind of triangle design on the diagram. The rising wedge has a solid bearish character. As such, the trigger side of the wedge example is the lower line. When you recognize a breakout through the lower level of a rising wedge, you ought to expect a sharp value drop equivalent to at any rate the size of the example. In this manner, breakouts through the lower level of a wedge are utilized for opening short positions. Itis what the rising wedge arrangement resembles:

Symmetrical Triangle Pattern

The even triangle is a circumstance on the graph where the highest points of the value activity are lower, and the bottoms are higher. Additionally, the different sides of the triangle are slanted with a similar point. This makes the balanced character of the triangle.

Ordinarily, with balanced triangle design, the normal directional breakout is obscure. The purpose behind this is bullish, and the bearish move has equivalent quality as observed through the value activity.

At the point when a breakout in the end happens, it is probably going to incite a value move equivalent to the size of the example. In this manner, you ought to deliberately distinguish a potential breakout in the upper and the lower level of the balanced triangle to take the exact situation in the market. The sketch underneath shows the equitable triangle development and conceivable breakout situations:

As you see from the model over, the potential objective depends on the size of the triangle development. With this kind of estimated move investigation, you will realize what's in store from the balanced triangle breakout, regardless of whether it breaks upwards, or downwards.

Hedges

Hedges on the diagram have a comparable shape to that of even triangles. They normally show up during patterns and have a pattern continuation character.

Bullish Pennant

The bullish pennant is like a balanced triangle in appearance, yet the Bullish hedge arrangement comes after a cost increment. Since hedges have pattern continuation character, the bullish hedge is probably going to proceed with the bullish pattern on the graph. At the point when the upper side of the hedge gets broken upwards, we are probably going to see an expansion equivalent to at any rate the size of the hedge, and normally bigger.

Thus when exchanging hedges, a subsequent objective ought to likewise be utilized to get a more significant move. When figuring the following goal, you would break down the value leg promptly following the hedge. You could set the objective to 1:1 of the past leg or .618 of that leg. At the point when the pattern appears to be stable and has a lofty slant, a 1:1 estimated move would be a suitable second target, and in every other case, the .618 of the leg could be utilized. How about we investigate the bullish hedge underneath:

See that here we have two targets. The red objective is the first, which is as large as the size of the fence. The green goal compares to the size of the past up move, which ought to be applied beginning from the upper side of the hedge.

Bearish Pennant

As you have most likely speculated, the bearish hedge is the equal representation of the bullish fence. Bearish hedges start with a value decline and end up with a balanced triangle appearance. Since hedges have pattern proceeding with character, bearish hedges are probably going to proceed with the bearish pattern.

At the point when the cost experiences the lower level of the bearish hedge, you should initially hope to catch the main objective, which is equivalent to the size of the fence itself. At the point when the value finishes this objective, you would then be able to attempt to get the further normal diminishing, which is equivalent to the size of the past leg or .618 of that leg. Allude to the picture underneath for a Bearish Pennant:

Expanding Triangle

You can scarcely ruin an extending triangle on the outline. The explanation behind this is it has one of a kind parameters. The two sides of the extending triangle are slanted, however, in inverse headings.

The course of the potential value move of this outline example is precarious to decide. In this way, we will currently present a couple of standards, which will assist you in identifying the heading of the average value moves.

Symmetrical Lines

And when the growing triangle is a flat, perfect representation of a balanced triangle, at that point, you should exchange the arrangement as a pattern continuation design. The picture beneath demonstrates a sketch of a growing triangle with stable lines:

Increasing Lines

If the different sides of the ever-increasing triangle are expanding, at that point, the example is probably going to have bearish characters.

Decreasing Lines

If the different sides of the extending triangle arrangement are diminishing, at that point, the figure is probably going to have bullish potentials.

One Side Stronger than the Other One

If the highest points of the cost activity are expanding, yet the bottoms are diminishing with a higher force, at that point, the example has bearish character. Despite what might be expected, if the bases are decreasing, yet the tops are expanding with a higher force, at that point, the example is probably going to have bullish character. As it were, you should exchange the heading of the side, which has a higher tendency.

Trading: Triangles in Forex

Since we have examined the greater part of the significant triangle designs in Forex, I will presently demonstrate to you how a triangle exchanging framework could function.

The diagram begins with a significant even triangle. The cost makes three diminishing tops and three expanding bottoms on the graph. The red bolt toward the start of the triangle estimates its size. As you see, a similar red flash is applied when the value breaks the upper degree of the triangle. The red glow demonstrates the potential objective of the example, which gets finished the following seven days.

Toward the finish of the bullish inclination, the value makes another balanced triangle. Later on, the amount gets through the lower level and finishes the size of the example (pink bolts).

While diminishing, the value activity makes a bearish hedge. This is the union after the primary motivation of the bearish pattern. The value breaks the lower level of the hedge subsequently. In transit down, we see the value finishing the main objective, which equivalents the size of the fence (red bolts). At that point, the lessening proceeds, and the decline is stretched out to a size equivalent to the last leg. (green pins).

The USD/CHF then makes a twofold base inversion example and changes to a bullish course. In transit up the value, activity makes a growing triangle design. Notice that both the lower and the upper level of the example are expanding. For this situation, the average value move is bearish and ought to be equivalent to the size of the case. Meanwhile, this time, the size of the matter is estimated from the closure side of the arrangement. The explanation behind this is we take the broadest side when we measure the standard move from the triangle breakout. The red bolts on the outline demonstrate to us that this example likewise finishes its objective.

Triangles are among the most significant diagram designs in Forex exchanging.

You have a contracting triangle on the outline when the tops and the bottoms of the value activity are pushing toward one another.

CHAPTER 7:

FUNDAMENTAL OR TECHNICAL ANALYSIS IN FOREX TRADING

As a trader, you can be confused about whether to opt for a technical or analysis, but it doesn't matter. As long as you learn the best time to enter or exit a trade, you can choose one or a combination of these analyses. But, before choosing any, you need to understand how both work and if they will assist you in making good trading decisions.

Fundamental analysis requires economic and statistical data too. Also, it uses data to determine currency strength. On the other hand, technical analysis use chat patterns to forecast price movements. Like flags and triangles. Well, read on to get insights on the similarities and differences between fundamental and technical analysis.

Fundamental Analysis

When it comes to figuring out whether currencies are going to strengthen or weaken, there are two styles of analysis that you will want to pay attention to. The first of these is what's known as "fundamental trading analysis", which is based on such things as economic reports and news.

Starting Point

A fundamental analysis is the best place to start, especially as you dip your toes in the trading waters. Before you do, though, you might want to consider how much you already know about the countries of the world and how they are governed. This is especially important in the countries whose currencies you plan to trade.

So, before you begin your daily analysis, make sure you create a clear mental picture of the countries you'll be trading on. How is their government structured and what are its cash reserves and deficits like? Create this as a starting point and then move on to your daily look at how things are changing.

Economic Reports

As a trader, you will want to stay updated on the economic reports coming out of not only the countries whose currencies you are directly trading, but also from the countries who are involved in trade with those countries. As we mentioned earlier, for example, the situation in the United States can have a big impact on the price of oil coming out of Canada, so it's going to affect the latter's economy.

You can take stock of a country's economy by looking at its inflation rate, employment rate and economic growth rate. In the case of employment, as a general rule the economy is improving if there are fewer people out of a job.

Be aware that there can also be seasonal impacts on this rate; for example, many businesses hire extra help for the holidays or for harvesting times. Conversely, you may see an uptick in layoffs when those events come to an end, which can skew the numbers. It's also important to be aware that the raw numbers aren't the only thing impacting the market: there is also the expectation of what those reports are going to show and the reaction of traders depending on whether it's as good or bad as expected.

If, for example, Canada was expected to release incredibly low unemployment numbers and the report reflects low unemployment not quite at the level expected, it can actually weaken the currency. If it showed even lower numbers than expected, this might cause worries about interest rate upticks, which will affect stocks and also impact the currency.

Inflation has a marked effect because it can indicate what's happening to the country's economy – but it can also be affected by growth rate. If the economy is growing, it often means there is a demand for currency, which means the currency is valued more but can also mean that inflation is rising and weakening that currency. These factors are linked so strongly that it's impossible to consider them separately.

Along with these reports, you should also pay attention to other aspects of the country's economy, such as interest rates. Short term rates tend to increase when the economy is strengthening and inflation is deemed likely to increase, while long term rates are affected by investment in government bonds. It's for this reason that currencies like the U.S. dollar are considered to be safe havens: their bond markets continue to do well even when less stable countries are suffering.

Supply and demand meanwhile play an important role: when it comes to international trade, prices change constantly based on how much of that commodity is available and how much is needed. The more people who want a good that's in limited supply, the higher the price will rise. Movements in funds between currencies will reflect this fact and will also affect the demand for those currencies.

Finally, it's important to be aware that most of the reports that have an influence on the Forex market are released at very specific times; the first Thursday of the month at 1 p.m. in your time zone, for instance. As you become more familiar with analysis, you'll start to learn when these dates and times occur and you'll come to expect them. This is incredibly important because the release of a report can have an instant impact on the market, so it should also be borne in mind when you initiate a trade.

For example, if you decide to initiate a trade on a Thursday evening but there's a report scheduled for 8 a.m. the next morning, the third Friday of the week, you might find that the report itself pushes the pips in the opposite direction to which you were expecting, scuppering your strategy in the process.

A quick search on the internet will show you that there are a number of free calendars available, some of which can be personalized to your needs such that you're only seeing the releases that will directly affect your trades and you're seeing them in local time. You can use these to your advantage by simply taking a quick look before initiating a trade to check whether there are any releases scheduled that may change what happens to the currency you're about to trade in.

You can also use them to remind yourself when those reports are looming – you can be among the first to check them when they release and can make trading decisions accordingly. For instance, you might find yourself closing trades, tightening stops or delaying a decision to initiate a trade.

News and Media

On a daily basis, you'll find news stories that have an impact on your Forex trading decisions. It's easy enough to root out stories that talk about government finances, the economy and large deals made by giant corporations, but you'll want to develop a filter as you sort through all that information.

Don't forget that "experts" can often be biased and stories may also reflect the hopes of the individual telling them or the government they represent. Thus the news can be remarkably helpful in developing your understanding of the world economic stage, but it's also important to remain skeptical of what's being said and find yourself as many sources as you are able to comfortably absorb in a day in order to verify, double check and ensure you're getting a clear picture.

International Events

While not technically a "source", it's worth mentioning international events in this chapter because of the immense influence they can have on your trading success.

Take a quick look at the headlines in the world's newspapers today and you'll see that huge events happen all the time. As a general rule, anything that causes fear and uncertainty is going to have a significant impact on the Forex market – and on your own individual trades, too. You can't see most of them coming, but you can prepare.

These massive events can include natural disasters such as earthquakes and hurricanes; conflict from wars or terrorism events; and human created disasters such as the meltdown of a nuclear reactor.

It's not uncommon for a country to shut down its markets when a massive events happen for the simple reason that panic can often lead to a crash. It's a way to ensure that cooler heads prevail before disaster strikes the financial markets.

When the market is shut, there's nothing you can do about your trades – they are frozen for the duration and your orders will not be fulfilled. The best way to avoid this from having a severe effect on your capital is to make sure you always leave stop-loss orders to automatically protect your position even when you can't do so yourself.

Looking for Economic Influencers

There are myriad influences on the market and they're all happening constantly, each one pushing the market up and down of their own accord while remaining just one part of the spider web and thus influenced in turn by other influences. Some of these influencers have global impacts and some will only affect certain aspects of a single country.

Let's take a closer look at some of the influencers you'll be sweeping for as you analyze the fundamentals:

Option Expirations

Be aware that funny things can happen on the monthly and quarterly expiration dates for the options market. Sellers will be aiming to secure certain price levels, which means volatility that can have a knock on effect. The upshot? Avoid these dates for new trades.

Statements from Officials

When officials from governments and banks make statements about the economy and financial situation, it can hold great weight with the marketplace. Watch out for press releases and even the minutes from meetings, as these can change the marketplace almost instantly, especially if they imply changes and movements that had not been foreseen.

Business Activities

When huge companies deal internationally, there is always a need for currency exchange. To acquire assets, even make big trading deals, one partner will need to exchange their local currency to pay the other partner. This temporarily changes how much cash is available in either currency, affecting demand and supply.

Market Ratings

Certain financial service companies are tasked with analyzing a country's finances and rating them accordingly. A triple-A rating ("AAA") means that the country has the capacity to meet its financial commitments; the lower the rating, the less they are believed able to do this. When ratings are released, they can significantly impact the economy of the country. A downgrade will have a negative impact, while an upgrade will have a positive impact.

Interventions

We've mentioned already that central banks in certain countries can be a lot more hands on than in others. In truth, most central banks are willing to get involved if the currency is spiraling in one direction or the other, though some more than others. It's worth knowing how hands on the central banks are in the countries you'll be dealing with, because an intervention will adjust the volatility and impact the currency dramatically.

Political Changes

The markets don't like uncertainty, and a change in leadership is very much a time of uncertainty. When a country votes in a new administration, it's impossible to be sure who will win that election and what policies they will aim to fulfill. For the most part, you'll find that the volatility increases for that currency while the election is ongoing and for a certain amount of time afterward, until the new administration has made its intentions clear.

The Bond Market

The bond market is a huge piece of the financial marketplace and as such has a big impact on trends in currencies. Informed traders like to stay abreast of what's happening in the bond market because the way money flows in and out of it correlates with what's happening in the currency market and can be very influential in pushing trends.

Monetary Policies

Central banks handle interest rates and the supply of money. Policies are used to maintain control over inflation and make sure the currency remains as stable as possible. It's arguably much easier to keep an eye on these policies and predict what they will do to the market because they are aimed directly at the markets, so they have clear aims that will have clearer effects on your trades.

Government Policies

Laws and regulations that a government puts in place can have a significant impact on the market. The objective of these policies tend to be directed towards keeping prices stable, making sure employment levels are as high as possible and promoting the economy. Be aware that there are many tools a government can employ to influence what's happening to the economy, from new tax policies to a policy that aims to increase business activities.

Analyzing an Economy

The many economies of the world are in a constant state of flux. You now know where to look to find out where in a cycle they currently are – and make trading decisions accordingly – but what do those cycles actually mean?

When boiled down to the basics, an economy is either going to be in a time of expansion or a time of recession. In the former case, there is an increase in economic activity and gross domestic product, which means more disposable income and thus spending, better employment levels and more demand.

A recession is basically the opposite and will see a drop in economic activity that has a blanket effect across internal markets for such things as housing and labor. If this gets bad enough or goes on for long enough, it becomes known as a depression.

Within those cycles you'll find inflation and deflation. Inflation refers to the prices being charged for items and services and usually rises when there is more demand than supply. Deflation, once again, is its opposite.

Gross domestic product refers to the overall value of those items and services that a single country generates over the course of one year. It's what the central banks tend to use to analyze the growth of the economy, which means it's also the best place to look to find out whether that country's economy is on the rise or on the decline.

It represents how much consumers are consuming, how much investment and government spending is going on and how much exporting is taking place.

Meanwhile, the "balance of payments" can tell you how healthy the economy is in comparison to others in the world, and it can do so fairly directly. It refers to all international activities and is considered to be in a good state when the country is accepting more payments from other countries than it is making.

The financial account will tell you how many international assets the country owns by looking at change in ownership. The country's budget deficit – the amount it must borrow above its income from taxes to meet the needs of its budget – will also indicate its internal economic health.

In general, what all these things will tell you is how risky the market is at the current moment. An economic decline is a time for safe bets, so it's usually when you'll find traders turning their attention to those safe currencies we discussed. In a time of increase, they will look more towards riskier currencies, which include the Canadian dollar, the Australian dollar, the New Zealand dollar, the British pound and the Euro.

Technical Analysis

Technical analysis is a theoretical framework used by Forex traders to study price movement. A trader can consider a historical price movement. You study the price pattern of a particular specific asset. Additionally, you use indicators, technical studies, and other analysis tools before embarking on a trade. You should check what happens and make a potential price movement. Charts are easy to visualize; you can see clearly how the market is fairing on. Additionally, you can view past data, current trends, and predicts what the future would be like.

Chart watching basics you should know;

Moving averages

Helps tin determine the overall trading. A trend condition usually, it plots the average price of a security in a particular period.

Price trends

Checks I stock price are accelerating or decelerating. And the amount of time and the period in which the price has stayed his way. Most chartists buy a security that is up in the trends.

Volume

Volume acts as lie detectors. With volume, one can predict how strong a trend influence may be. Decreasing volume indicates that a trend can be on the verge of a reversal.

Appear above or below a chart.

All the information on a current market is reflected on a price. When you know the history of the trading market, you will be able to make great trading decisions.

It acts as a map, guiding you on how to curate or conduct a trade. Technical analysis was self-fulfilling as it's subjective. Technicians use various methods to study the price patterns. That is;

Technical analysis candle- candle patterns show high, low, open, and close levels. With this, you can get clues on how the buyers and sellers reacted during the previous years.

Technical analysis chart - the chart gives clarity to buyers and sellers throughout the market.

Technical analysis indicators- using this chart as trade will help you understand the market conditions. You will also view the rising and the falling momentums of the market

Importance of a Technical Analysis

There are many uncertainties in this market. But as a trader, you have to take a risk and work on probabilities. As much as the market can be chaotic, you will identify patterns and make the most out of it. With a clear review of the charts, and study of the market, you have the potential of making the correct choices when it comes to your trade. You will know when to enter a market. And, the most important thing is, you learn how to get out of a trade and when. Secondly, you learn to identify patterns mark can figure out what to do when particular issues arise in the market. Also, you get to learn to determine the probabilities and jump into the right opportunities, when odds work on your favor.

How do you conduct a technical analysis?

Determine which security interests you -For instance, you can do research on which sector is at the moment trading this will assist in deciding on what to buy or sell Choose a strategy that suits you -each stock is unique. And each cannot utilize the same approach.

Choose a trading account. To maximize profits, go for the account with the right functionality, cost, and also support.

Comprehend your tools -Knowing thee tools that fit your trading strategies and tools is essential. Free tools are available for you to learn and understand the features. Try out to test your system with the market data before jumping on the bandwagon of trading. Choose a few indicators that can fit the technical indicator requirements you chose. Monitor how they perform each day.

Advantages of technical analysis

You learn when to exist and enter a trade- through the patterns in charts; you will learn how to jump out of a trade.

They provide you with the right information directions are essential to in any field. Technical analysis offers precisely what you need to navigate this industry. Get information on the current trends- prices tend to increase or decrease. Usually, they reflect on the information of an existing asset to make decisions.

Differences between fundamental and technical analysis

As much as the two analysis help you get trading results. They have numerous differences. Some are here below

Fundamental analysis uses economic m reports of industry statistics and news events to analyze data and make predictions; also, it forecasts share prices on the basis company statics and economic industry. Technical analysis uses a chart to analyze data and majorly focuses on internal data and market statistics.

Fundamental analysis is concerned with the investments. The investors usually hold or buy a stock of a company with the information got. Technical analysis is more concerned with the trade.

The security of the future prices us determine by the past and present performance a company make in Forex trading, while indicators and charts are the ones that determine the future market prices

A long-term trader usually utilizes fundament analysis. Long term investors buy stocks containing enormous dividends pay-out and regularly release or sell them after several years when the stocks have passed through several fluctuations while short berm traders usually utilize technical analysis. Such traders o did not buy or keep goods for years, but instead, they focus more on short term profits. Fundamental utilizes the intrinsic value of stock got when one analyses income statements like cash flow management, profit margins, and returns on equity. They predict the future of the market. A technical analysis, depend on a chart, technical indicators, resistance, and support to analyze future trend patterns. In fundamental analysis, no assumptions are made while assumptions like similar price trends are not news, in technical analysis Fundamentals analysts don't need to go back to history to find to discover past prices and the fluctuations incurred. However, technicians trade re-occurs, and the possibility of history repeating itself is high.

So which analysis techniques should you choose?

Most analysis on street walls prefers fundamental analysis to technical analysis. Both technical and fundamental have their advantages and disadvantages. But a good investor will point out that their combination of both the two, end up producing t exceptional results.

Risk management

Knowledge of both fundamental and technical approach can help to handle any risk involved in a trade. Economic can tell if the attitude of particular market changes, but fails to inform you when the view of the market is wrong. Technical analysis helps you manage risk as you can view on the charts and can help you revise a market view.

Also, a combination of the two analyses can confirm specific trends. When, most people in a country expect a higher interest rate, but it doesn't manifest, then that countries' currency would likely decrease in value. Furthermore, When the currency continues rising, there could be a possibility of other factors involved rather than the interest rate. A technical trader can use the way markets reacts to fundamental news to their advantage

Partying shots

When marketers try to focus on future price movements, they use fundamental analysis to look at issues such as political developments and economic data.; they use technical analysis to read charts and interpret price movements or instead come the two. That what, you need to do a trader.

CHAPTER 8:

CURRENCY PAIRS

Among the 160 different currencies circulating in different parts of the world, there are only handfuls that are actively exchanged in the Forex market. Most of them are only exchanged in the territories where they are used. The current Forex market actively trades in only around 17 currencies based on their liquidity and the number of exchanges made between those currencies. These so-called major currencies account for over 90 percent of all the money exchanged in the foreign currency exchange market.

Similar to company stocks in the stock market, currencies are assigned three-letter abbreviations, set by the International Standards Organization. This greatly simplifies the quoting and trading of these currencies in the world market. When trading these currencies, the quote for these trades is always shown in pairs. Each currency fluctuates relative to other currencies, which is why they are traded in pairs. Out of the active major currencies, there are hundreds of potential currency combinations. However, there are about 100 pairs that are commonly traded, with around 50 pairs actively being used by international Forex brokers.

In Forex trading, exotic currencies are generally paired with major currencies. It is doubtful that a non-major currency will be paired with another non-major currency. As an example, it would be challenging to find an exchange that trades the Uruguay Peso and the Iraqi dinar. However, finding an exchange that trades those currencies with the US dollar is relatively easy. Some companies and individuals do exotic trade pairs with another, but their volume merely is just too small for international brokers.

Currency Quotations

The International Organization for Standardization submitted ISO 4217 in 1978. The standard assigned three-letter codes to represent individual currencies to be used in any application for trading, banking, and commerce. It was also agreed upon that the three-letter alphabetic codes for International Standard ISO 4217 would be used in international trading. The list of codes is also frequently updated, as new currencies emerge and older ones are discontinued.

When it comes to Forex trading, currencies always come in pairs. As an example, a trade made with the US dollar versus the euro would look like this (USD/EUR). The US dollar versus the Canadian dollar would look like this (USD/CAD). It goes without saying that a currency can never be traded without itself.

The first currency indicated in the quotation is called the base currency, while the second one is referred to as the counter currency. A numerical value is assigned to the currency pair that may be up to 4 decimal places. The last decimal place is referred to as a "pip." The value assigned to currency pairs is the amount of the counter currency required to buy one unit of the base currency. As an example, if the USD/CAD is quoted at 1.32, it means that it would currently require 1.32 Canadian dollars to buy one single US dollar. On trading platforms, these values would fluctuate in real-time as the value of each currency varies depending on the market.

There are very many types of currencies across the world, and all of them have three letter symbols, for example, the Euros are EUR, American Dollar are USD, British Pounds are GBP, Swiss Francs are CHF, etcetera. The currencies have been majorly divided into two major and minor currencies. The major currencies involve these derived from the powerful economies in the world that are; the USA, the UK, Japan, the Eurozone, Australia, Canada, New Zealand, and Switzerland. These currencies create forex pairs with each other and with other minor currencies.

When one goes to a store to purchase some groceries or any other item, he/she needs to exchange one asset of value for another for instance milk for money. This applies for forex exchange too; buying and selling one currency for another. Every pair involves two currencies whereby one buys or sells the currencies against the other.

Forex pairs can be classified into three types namely Major pairs, Exotic pairs, and Minor pairs. The major pairs always consist of the United States Dollar and many people trade in them. The major pairs are USDCHF, USDJPY, EURUSD, AUDUSD, GBPUSD, NZDUSD, and USDCAD. The minor pairs involve all the currencies participating in the major pairs apart from the United States Dollar. They include CHFJPY, EURGBP, EURAUD, JPYAUD, NZDCAD et cetera. The exotic pairs involve one minor currency and one major currency, for instance, USDNOK, USDKSH, EURTRY etcetera.

Prices are always in terms of the price of one currency relative to another. Learning how to read and understand quoted data is important, and you need to have a thorough understanding of what everything is referring to. The good thing is that this is not really very complicated, so most readers will pick it up in a short amount of time.

Currency Pair Trading

When you are trading currency, you are trading one currency against another. So, what does this mean? Essentially, you buy one currency and sell the other simultaneously.

You need to understand how you would buy or sell currency pairs based on the market conditions that you are anticipating. Let's use the Euro and US Dollar currency pair as an example.

Currencies are priced relative to one another, and they are always quoted in pairs. For example, the Euro and the US Dollar are one of the currency pairs. Currency pairs are ordered, and the ordering is always the same. For the Euro and the US

Dollar, it will appear like this:

EUR/ USD

The currency on the left side is the primary, or base currency.

The currency on the right side is the secondary. The order never changes, this is just the standard, and it's for trading and ordering purposes only. So you will not see USD/ EUR quoted. It does not have anything to do with one currency value versus another or anything of the sort. The ordering of the pairs has the practical significance that we described above. So if you want to buy Euros because you think that the Euro is going to go up with respect to the dollar, then you buy EUR/ USD. Or consider the pair GBP/ AUD, which pairs the Great British Pound and the Australian Dollar. If you think that the Great British pound is going to go up against the Australian Dollar, then you would buy the currency pair. That means you are buying Great British Pounds and selling Australian Dollars. On the other hand, if you believe that the Great British Pound is going to go down with respect to the Australian Dollar, then you would sell the currency pair, meaning that you're selling Great British Pounds and buying Australian dollars.

Many of these currencies are referred to by nicknames that are of historical origin. It's good to know what these nicknames are in case you get involved with conversations about currency trading, as experienced traders may throw around this terminology. You would not want to be lost in a conversation because you didn't know what the nicknames are. You may also on occasion see the nicknames used in articles and such.

Some of the nicknames are obvious. The Australian dollar is often referred to in shorthand form as the Aussie. The US Dollar is known as the greenback. This name will not surprise anyone. The New Zealand dollar sometimes goes by the name Kiwi.

A couple of more obscure names exist as well. The Great British Pound, while sometimes known by the name pound sterling, also gets referred to by some as the cable. The origin of its term is moderately interesting. In the days when electronic communications networks were first being established, the name cable came about because trading was done by undersea cables between the U.S. and Great Britain, and so American bankers began referring to the Pound as the cable. Somehow this name has stuck through more than 100 years of usage. Another interesting name is for the Canadian dollar, which sometimes gets referred to as the Loonie. This comes from the name of the dollar coin that the country used to have with a duck on one side of the coin.

The Majors

The currencies of the main developed countries and the European Union are known as the "majors." These include the US Dollar, the Euro, the Japanese Yen, the Swiss Franc, the Australian dollar, the New Zealand dollar, the Canadian dollar, and the Great British Pound. The symbols used for these are USD, EUR, JPY, CHF, AUD, NZD, CAD, and GBP, respectively.

But when someone says the "majors" they are really talking

about the currency pairs that these are involved in. The major currency pairs include:

EUR/ USD

USD/ JPY

GBP/ USD

USD/ CAD

USD/ CHF

AUD/ USD

NZD/ USD

The majors make up the vast majority of the trading on the Forex markets. But as you might imagine, there are many different currency pairs. In fact, they can number 100 currency pairs. There can be money to made trading currencies that are not majors. You have to be careful when looking at other currency pairs because you might find yourself in a liquidity trap.

You know from finance that liquidity is a measure of how quickly you can convert an asset into cash. Something that is readily converted into cash is highly liquid.

Therefore, a gold bar is pretty liquid, you can run down to a precious metals store and sell it for cash right away. A house is less liquid. While it can be converted into cash, it might take some time to sell it. When the markets are hot, it might sell in a few days or weeks, but it could take months at other times. If you needed money to pay for a car repair, selling your house would not be a good strategy, but selling a gold bar would allow you to raise the money nearly immediately. In the currency markets, liquidity means you can either buy back a currency pair (if you sold it to open your position) or you can sell it (if you bought it to open) quickly. As we will see, when you are watching currency pairs on the charts, the time frame over, which you may need to make a move to close your position, can be very small. So it's important to be able to move quickly. Many people, including some experts that you might run into on the internet, might be promoting the idea that you can make money trading minor currencies, like the Mexican Peso. There is a lot of software out there that will find currency pairs that are trending for you. That is all well and good, except it's not so good if you are trying to enter a trade when you identify it forming, and it takes so long that by the time your order is filled, it's nearing the peak in a price increase.

Alternatively, you might be following a trend, and it starts showing signs that the trend is coming to a reversal. That is the time to get out of the trade. But you might get in a situation where you can't close your position quickly because it's a currency pair with low liquidity. For that reason, you might want to stay away from minor currencies. The action is in the majors, and one thing about the majors is you won't have to worry about the kinds of problems that I have just described.

Liquidity also impacts the cost of trading. The less liquid a currency pair is, the higher the cost of trading it. There are currency pairs that involve some of the currencies from developed countries, which do have relatively high trading volume. These are composed of the major currencies when they are paired with each other but not with the US dollar.

Next, we come to the so-called "exotics." These are currency pairs between a major and a strong economy that isn't considered one of the majors. So the USD or Euro can be paired with each of these currencies. Some of the "exotics" include Sweden, Norway, Singapore, Hong Kong, Denmark, South Africa, and Turkey. The exotics are not traded as much and so can be considered to be illiquid. As a beginning trader, they are probably best avoided. Some currency pairs that you will see include the Mexican Peso (MXN) and the Chinese currency (sometimes called the Yuan) CNH.

It doesn't end there, of course; you can trade currencies for nearly every country on earth that has one, so, for example, you could trade the Mexican Peso in one of its currency pairs. However, these currency pairs may be illiquid as well. As long as you can get in and out of the trade quickly, it's considered to be a good currency pair.

Summary: How Currency Pairs Work

Let's set up a hypothetical or generic currency pair to review the basic concepts. (currency one) / (currency two)

When you say you are buying the currency pair, that means you are buying currency one and selling currency two. You will do this if you believe that currency one will rise in value with respect to currency two. Or put another way, you believe that currency two is going to drop in value, relative to currency one. The currency pair is always quoted in this manner. If you believe that currency two is going to rise in value with respect to currency one, then you would sell the currency pair. This is a bet that currency one is going to decline in value relative to currency two. If the currency pair in question was EUR/ CAD, buying the pair means you are betting on the Euro, and selling the pair means you are betting on the CAD. It might sound a little bit like we are beating a dead horse, but this concept is important. Let's think about how this is going to work out in a chart. The Forex market will let you look at charts of currency pairs, and they look a lot like stock market charts. But it's important to understand the direction of the curve since we are talking about pairs.

If we have a chart for A/ B, then if the curve is going up, that indicates an increasing price for the currency pair A/ B. And what that means is that currency A is increasing in value, while currency B is decreasing in value. If you had bought the currency pair A/ B, then this would be a winning trade for you. On the other hand, if the curve was going downward, this would be favorable for currency B – indicating that it was going up while currency A was going down in value.

Remember that everything is relative when it comes to

currency trading, there are not absolutes. So, it's all about the price of once currency relative to another. That may or may not impact other currency pairs. Here is an example: the chart below is for the AUD/ USD currency pair. On the left-hand side, the price is decreasing, by a lot, but on the right-hand side, it made a steep climb upwards. Using what we just learned, you realize that on the left side of the chart, the value of the Australian Dollar was decreasing relative to the US Dollar, or you could put it in terms of saying the US dollar is increasing relative to the Australian Dollar. So on the left-hand side of the chart, if you had bought the currency pair, you probably would not have been too happy at that point. But if you had sold the currency pair – and therefore favored the US Dollar, for that time frame your bet was favored. Meanwhile on the right side of the chart, as the curve is moving upward, if you had bought the currency pair, you'd be happy because an upward trend of the pair means that it was increasing in value – the Australian dollar was rising against the US Dollar. If you had sold the pair, well, in this case, you were losing money.

The price of the pair is listed on the right-hand side. This means one Australian dollar is worth $ 0.69 in US dollars. You can invert that (1/ 0.69) to express how many Australian dollars a US dollar would buy; the answer is 1.45.

Principles and Characteristics of Currencies

Currency exchange has been in place for a long time now. And by a long time, we are not talking about a couple of hundred years or even a few thousand years. We are referring to the BC period. More specifically, to around 10,000 BC. The only difference was that at that time people used the barter system to exchange goods and services. But this created feelings of dissatisfaction among the traders. How can one gauge the value of objects? Even if they were referring to a specific object, how can they say that the object from one place is better than another? For example, let us assume that you were providing two bags of rice for a fine carpet. (I"m not sure if this was the exchange rate, but let's pretend that it is. Though if you are giving two bags of rice for a carpet, then that carpet better fly!) Now, you know that in your little village or town, carpets are of the finest quality. But does that mean all the carpets around the world have the same quality? Does that mean you are getting a fair return for your two bags of rice? Now imagine this scenario playing out between the countries. How can one set accurate values for each country's "currencies"? How can exchanges take place that are fair and governed by the right rules?

This situation created a system of bias and prejudice. This started to disrupt whatever form of economy was used during those times.

Eventually, the earliest coins were made in parts of what we now refer to as Turkey. Empires and nations around the world began to manufacture their own coins using precious materials like gold and silver.

This controlled the chaos of exchanges that took place

between traders because everything had a proper value. If you are going to purchase something, you knew how much you had to pay for it.

Fast forward to the 19th century. More specifically, to the year 1847. Up until now, countries were commonly utilizing gold and silver to make international payments. But that changed with the introduction of the Gold Standard Monetary System. With this system in place, the paper currencies of the countries had a value directly linked to gold. This means that a certain value of money from a country could be converted into a specific amount of gold, depending on that country's currency value.

Over time, this system was dropped in order to give each country a degree of autonomy when managing their affairs. This means that each country is responsible for creating their own currencies without leveraging it against anything. When governments began issuing their own paper currencies that were not attached to a physical commodity like gold or silver, that currency was given the term "fiat money".

Why is this significant? As we had seen, autonomy.

But once again, what does this actually mean?

With the presence of fiat money, the value of the money is dependant on the relationship between the supply and demand of the country along with the stability of the government. Rather than using gold and silver to decide the value of the money, the situation of the country would derive the value of the money.

Enter World War II.

And once again, it started with chaos.

The whole world was experiencing unprecedented levels of chaos. Governments were scrambling to find a solution to stabilize the economies of the world. They turned their eyes to the U.S. dollar.

In order to provide a solution, the Bretton Woods Agreement was established. According to this agreement, the U.S. dollar was set as the exchange rate for gold, giving nations around the world one currency to work with when managing international trades. Other currencies were eventually pegged against the U.S. dollar.

Once again, another solution to control the chaos of exchanges was formed. But did it last? Sadly, no.

History has a strange habit of repeating itself. Because even the Bretton Woods Agreement became obsolete as it became apparent that countries progressed at different speeds. In fact, it was observed that new rules introduced in countries could change trade laws and currency values.

In 1971, the Bretton Woods Agreement was dropped. The world needed a different system of currency valuation.

The U.S. was once again placed in the pilot seat and with the country's guidance, a free-floating market was introduced that would actually determine the exchange value of currencies based on the demand and supply in a particular country.

Of course, this innovative way of looking at currencies brought with it a whole new set of problems, the most prominent being the fact that it was not always easy to establish fair exchange rates. Additionally, gathering information about a country and its governmental policies, domestic situations, and trade policies could not be done quickly enough.

Then came the 1990s, a time we should all be thankful for. After all, it was because of the internet boom that we now have access to Facebook, online multiplayer RPGs, Netflix, and YouTube.

One of the greatest achievements of the internet was the availability of information instantly to anyone, anywhere in the world. The foundation provided by the internet allowed people to create new and innovative technologies.

These innovations led to the establishment of various trading platforms.

As we saw earlier, prior to the availability of trading platforms, the Forex market was simply something only certain entities or individuals with high net worth could access. It was never really available to everyone and the thought of joining it probably meant you had to have a million dollars, take a loan, perform an ancient ritual to the god of money, and maybe even sacrifice a few goats.

It was like a realm that everyone wanted to be in but no one had any access to.

CHAPTER 9:

PROVEN STRATEGIES FOR FOREX TRADING

Strategy 1: Hull Moving Average

The Hull moving average is a more sophisticated moving average. Like the exponential moving average, it uses price weighting to give more weight to recent prices when it computes the moving average. It is a surprisingly accurate moving average, and it will give you a nice smooth curve that seems to pass right through the centers of the candlesticks on your chart. If you want, you can use the Hull moving average in place of the exponential moving average for any strategy, but this type of strategy seems to work best when you are using one-day candlesticks. So it's going to be best suited for swing and position traders (or end of day traders as well) when looking for points to enter and exit your positions.

The strategy is the same as with other moving averages. That is, you are going to want to look for points, where a short period moving average crosses a moving average that has a longer period. If you are looking into a swing or position trading strategy, you are going to want to use longer periods. As an aside, when you use the longer periods the Hull moving average is not going to fit through the middles of the candlesticks, that happens for a nine period or less moving average.

For this case, using the Hull moving average for a longer time frame, you are going to want to set up a 50-period Hull moving average and an 80-period Hull moving average. The idea here is to look for the usual crossings and confirm by checking for reversal signals in the candlesticks.

Let's consider a buy signal first. Looking for a buy signal, there has been some sort of downtrend. You are keeping your eye open for the 50-period moving average to cross above the 80-period moving average. When it does so, then you are going to want to look at the candlesticks. If you see an uptrend or bullish signal in your candlesticks, then this is a definite signal to buy a currency pair.

Now consider that the currency pair A/ B has been in an uptrend. You may have either bought the currency pair A/ B, and you are looking for the right time to close your trade by selling it. Alternatively, you could be looking for an opportunity to sell to open the A/ B currency pair, so that you can bet on currency B against currency A.

The first thing you are going to look for is the crossing over of the lines. When you are in an uptrend, you should be seeing the short period moving average above the long-term moving average. When it crosses below, this is when you get ready to either close your position, if you had previously bought the A/ B currency pair, or you are looking to sell to open. Either way, confirm the signal by checking the candlesticks. If it confirms that downtrend has been starting, then you can go ahead and make your move.

The Hull moving average method is not restricted to longer-term trading. You can use a shorter-term scenario with the Hull moving average. For example, if you are intraday trading, you could use a 9 period Hull moving average and a 20 period Hull moving average with 5-minute candlesticks.

Strategy 2: Supertrends

Supertrend is an indicator that you can use on your charts, combining trend information with volatility data. Using this strategy, you will use two exponential moving averages. These will be the five-period exponential moving average, and the 20-period exponential moving average. As usual, you want to look for cross overs. When the five-period moving average crosses above the 20-period moving average, this is an indicator that an uptrend is coming.

Conversely, when the five-period moving average moves below the 20-period moving average, this tells us that a downtrend is coming. Then you want to combine this signal with the supertrend indicator. The supertrend indicator is going to be color-coded, either green or red. If it turns green and you see the five-period moving average crossing to the upside, this is a buying signal, so you will want to buy your currency pair at this point.

On the other hand, if the five-period moving average crosses below the 20-period moving average, and the super trend indicator turns red, this is a sell signal. Therefore, if you see this signal, then you will sell your currency pair. Super trends are very popular among Forex traders.

Strategy 3:The Floor Trader Strategy

The floor trading method is primarily a swing trading strategy, but it can be used for day trading as well. If you plan to use the floor trader strategy, you will rely on 9 periods, and 18-period exponential moving averages, and look for the 9-period moving average to cross below the 18-period moving average to signal a downtrend, and hence give a sell signal. Alternatively, you will look for the 9-period moving average to cross above the 18-period moving average to indicate an uptrend, which will be a signal to buy a currency pair. Then wait for a few candlesticks to pass to confirm that the trend is holding and that the candlesticks are showing no signs of reversal. Then you want to wait for a retracement before entering the trade. In a downtrend, this will allow you to sell at a relatively high price because a retracement is a temporary move upward in price before it resumes the longer-term downtrend.

Now let's consider the opposite situation. That is, we are going to look at an upward trend in price. This time, a retracement is doing to be a small drop in price before the trend resumes. So when the lines cross with the short-term moving average going above the long-term moving average, then you look for three candlesticks to go by to confirm that the trend is not going to reverse. Then wait for the retracement, and buy when the price dips to the relatively low.

The time frame depends on your time frame as a trader. So the candlesticks could be one-minute candlesticks if you are scalping, or 1 hour or even 1-day candlesticks if you are swing or position trading.

Strategy 4: Gartley Fibonacci Patterns

A Gartley pattern is a tool used to look for a retracement. This is when a temporary, and relatively small reversal happens before the overall trend resumes. What you want to look for as a pattern forming on the price chart that resembles the letter M.

So the price will rise up, then drop down but not all the way down to the previous price level, rise up again, and drop down again. It's not going to be an ideal "M" shape, but instead, it will probably come up not quite as high on the second peak, and the last point is going to be higher than the first point on the far left. Wait for the pattern to appear on the chart. Then you want to check the candlestick patterns and see if there is a bullish reversal signal. Then you want to buy a currency pair at a price level that is 2 pips higher than the high price of the most recent bullish candlestick. To protect yourself in the event of a reversal, you can put a 5 pip stop loss order below the last closing price of the final bearish candlestick.

When using this technique to sell a currency pair, you look for the same setup but look for a bearish reversal pattern. Then you look to sell at 2 pips below the low price of the most recent bearish candlestick, and buy if the price goes 2-5 pips above the last high price seen in the chart.

Strategy 5: Bollinger Band Trading Strategy

Bollinger bands are a tool available on any trading platform. They provide you with a wealth of information, including a dynamic estimate of support and resistance. This is done using a 20-period moving average, which will display as the "middle" Bollinger band. The standard deviation, one above and one below (or many people use two standard deviation widths) form the upper and lower Bollinger bands. If the trend of the middle band is upward, then this is a buy signal. If the trend is downward, this is a selling signal. When you add Bollinger bands to a chart, you are going to see the price fluctuating about the middle Bollinger band, and going near (or slightly exceeding) the upper and lower Bollinger bands which mark out current levels of price support and resistance. To make a move, if the trend is upward and the price comes back and touches the middle Bollinger band, then buy your currency pair. On a downtrend, if the price rises back to touch the middle Bollinger band, then this is your sell signal.

Strategy 6: Cci Moving Average Strategy

You can use the CCI oscillator for the same purpose. With a CCI moving average strategy, you will use two exponential moving averages together with the CCI oscillator. Typically, a 7-period exponential moving average and a 14-period exponential moving average are used. To enter a selling position, you look for a crossover, of the 7-period moving average to move below the 14-period moving average. Don't make a move immediately; you want to make sure that there is not going to be a rally that reverses the trend lines a second time. If the downtrend is confirmed, look for overbought conditions in the CCI. If you see overbought conditions, then it's a good time to sell a currency pair. For buying conditions, you will look for the formation of an upward trend. The first signal is going to be the 7-period exponential moving average crossing above the 14-period exponential average. Check the CCI for oversold conditions, and when you see that and confirm that there is not going to be a resumption of the downtrend, you buy your currency pair. This is good to use with the majors. You should also incorporate candlestick analysis to confirm your signals.

Strategy 7: Trendline Trading

This procedure can form the basis of a Forex strategy that can be used on any time frame that suits you. At a minimum, you need to have two dips for an upward trend or two peaks for a downward trend. Once you have drawn the trendline, you wait for the price to touch the trend line a third time. You can buy 2-5 pips above a high point or sell 2-5 pips below a low point.

Strategy 8: Channel Breakout

These are the trends that will break out of the resistance and support curve, and often, they show up after a new event, or a piece of news is released. This is where you will want to bring in your knowledge of the economy so that you can determine when a breakout is going to occur. If you guess correctly, you can get into the market before the price goes up and sell when it reaches its top. Or you can get out of the market in time if the news is bad or brings up uncertainty before the market crashes and you lose out on all your money.

Many traders find that working with a technical analysis can be a great option to help them earn a good amount of money on the Forex market. It does require looking at a lot of charts and graphs to see success. But for those who can learn about the trends that occur with a specific currency, and who are willing to watch out for some big news items that may change the course of their currency pair away from its historical values, then a technical analysis may be the right option for you. Fibonacci Indicators And Applying Them

There are ways to understand in case your currency trading strategy is excellent or successful.

- Start knowing how effective it has been in the past. It will pay to learn simply how much previous or current users associated with the operational system have received so far by utilizing the strategy. Regardless of that, additionally obtain some informative data on how much is the drawdown that is maximum of system in its previous trading.

- There was a win-loss ratio which it is possible to check. It is about how much you have won compared with much you have actually lost. Apart from that, there is also a profit-loss ratio. This s about the average winning trade set alongside the trade that is losing.

- You would also need to know how consistent the system is in delivering earnings. Horizontal Levels And The 'Swing Points'

This is going to involve liberal use of math, so you should be prepared. Actually, here is the perfect moment to add in a little advice. If you are not comfortable with pips and lots, then don't jump in on a trade. Try to familiarize yourself with these terms and the way they work. This is because when you finally start trading, you should be aware of the changes happening to the currency on every level. With that small recommendation, let us move on.

I am going to use the fourth decimal point system for the example below. If you can understand it, then you can apply the same calculation to a five-decimal-point system as well.

We have now established that EUR/ USD shifted from 1.1183 to 1.1184. Therefore, currently, EUR/ USD = 1.1184 or in other words, 1 EUR to 1.1184 USD. We represent this as 1 EUR/ 1.1184 USD.

We simply have to replace the above components with values.

We know for certain the following: The amount of change in the value of the counter currency is 0.0001 USD. The rate of exchange is 1 EUR/ 1.1184 USD.

In the end, we are looking at the following value: [0.0001 USD] × [1 EUR/ 1.1184 USD]

We can shift the values around so that the equation looks like the following: [0.0001 USD/ 1.1184 USD] × 1 EUR

This gives us the following value:

0.00008941344 EUR

The above value of the euro is what you get for every one unit that you trade.

Now let us assume that you have chosen to pick up a mini-lot of 10,000 units of the EUR/ USD. When there is a single change of pip in the exchange rate of the currencies, then the entire change in the value would be 10,000 units × 0.00008941344 EUR. This would give us roughly 0.89 EUR change in the position of the value of the currency exchange.

Of course, the keyword to remember is "roughly" as every time the exchange rate shifts, so does the value of each pip.

The above example is just a simple explanation of the way pips work. When you are working with the forex market, you might have to make a note of the values in order to make the best trade.

Strategy 9: Conservative

This strategy simply encourages that you should be conservative in your approach. Avoid trades that are aggressive, especially those that lack sufficient research. The key to this approach is to make small but multiple trades. Instead of focusing on how much you can earn from every trade, you should focus on increasing your rate of success. The idea behind this approach is that once you are able to establish an effective strategy, then you can always increase the amount that you trade with. As a beginner, what is important is for you to work on a powerful strategy that can give you a high rate of success. Be as conservative as possible and never commence a trade that uses more than 5% of your total funds. The key is to stay low and let your small yet continuous gains turn into a significant profit. Also, by remaining conservative, you will not be provoked to turn into an emotional trader. This is also an excellent strategy to stay longer in the market. It is also strongly suggested if it is your first time to trade in a real forex market using real money. Be as conservative as possible and cut back on your risks and losses. Last but not least, keep your focus on making continuous small profits. Being consistent is the key. Once you are able to establish a good flow of profits and if you are already confident enough in your strategy, then that is the time for you to increase the amount that you invest per trade. Still, be sure not to use more than 5% of your total funds per trade.

Strategy 10:Go with the flow

Sometimes the best way to trade is simply to go with the flow. The key to this is simply to be updated on the news. If the US economy is doing really well, then you may want to start going long on it, especially if the economy of the other currency is not showing any development. You simply have to see which one is going strong in the market. You can also apply this using technical analysis. If you see a strong price movement, then you can take advantage of it. Still, when you use this approach, no matter what strategy you use, you should apply fundamental analysis in order to significantly increase your chances of making a profit. If you do not want to make any research, you might want to read the posts on forex trading forums and see how the traders respond. Sometimes you may be able to spot interesting ideas and profitable opportunities. However, just make sure not to rely completely on whatever you read from other people. It is still important for you to develop your own understanding of the forex market.

Strategy 11:Reversal trading

As its name already suggests, this is where you expected a reversal in the price trend, and your objective here is to make an entrance into a trade that is ahead of the market. This is not really a strategy for beginners as it requires you to have more understanding of how the market moves. Reversals do not always occur but they can be highly profitable if you are able to take advantage of them. There are tools that traders use in order to identify a reversal, such as visual cues, as well as volume and momentum indicators.

Strategy 12:Retracement

The concept behind this strategy is that prices do not move in a straight line especially during highs and lows. Instead, they usually make a pause or only change in the middle of a larger path. Hence, when you apply retracement, you will wait for the price to "retrace" itself or pull back. This is to confirm that a pattern is being made. Once you are able to identify this, then you can make use of the pattern that is being formed by taking appropriate actions. When trading currencies, knowing the most probable movement of the price in a graph is a big advantage that can lead to profit.

Strategy 13:Forex wedge breakout

There are many breakout strategies. With this one, what you are looking for is a wedge pattern where the price goes up and down. However, unlike a usually wedge, you will see that the differences between the price increase and decrease gets smaller over time. You will know that if the pattern continues then it will soon to an end and become a mere horizontal line. The key is to take advantage of this pattern before it disappears. So, you should open a position just immediately after a price decrease. Keep in mind that you should not hold on to the position for so long; otherwise, you will more likely experience a bad loss. To be safe, stay conservative. Once you make a profit by a few pips, close down your position. How much you will profit will depend on the behavior of the pattern, but it will most likely be lower than the previous increase in value. Be sure to take advantage of this opportunity and close your position while still at a profit.

Strategy 14:Pin bar strategy

This is a strategy that you can apply when you are using technical analysis. You can easily identify the right time to use this strategy by looking at a graph. The signal is when you see a horizontal line which means that the price fluctuations have been stagnant over some time. This horizontal line is what is referred to as the **bullish pin bar**. The concept behind this theory is that the resistance will serve as a new support for a price increase. Hence, if you make an investment at any point in the bullish pin bar, then you will most likely experience a profit in the very near future. Hence, when you see a bullish pin bar, you should consider entering the market and opening a position depending on the currency pair where it applies. Take note that this does not work 100% of the time. However, there is a good chance that it will turn out to be a good investment. A better approach is to spot for a bullish pin bar and make some more research before investing your money in a trade. This way you will be more confident and also increase your chances of making the right trading decision.

Strategy 15:Averaging down

Averaging down is an effective way to invest in a currency pair at a bargain price. It is also a good way to earn a high amount of profit. However, it is considered an aggressive approach, so be cautious of using this strategy. The key to this strategy is to identify as currency pair that you think would be profitable in the near future. You then invest in that currency pair. Let us say that the price drops and you experience some losses, instead of closing your position, you should make another investment in the same currency pair. Since the price has also dropped, then the cost of the pair will now also be lower. Continue to do this as the price of the currency pair decreases. Okay, although this may seem like a losing strategy at first, it can actually turn out to be highly profitable after some time. Just imagine what will happen if its price finally reverses and increases back either to its original value when you first applied this strategy, or higher. As you can see, all your open positions will experience a nice profit. This is an effective and highly profitable strategy. The important thing is to be able to identify a currency pair that would be profitable in the near future and then hold on to it. To do this, you may want to research as much as you can about the currencies involved in a pair, so that you can have a better understanding of how likely their prices are going to change in the next few days or weeks. Although this strategy seems very practical and highly profitable, it is noteworthy that you should be very careful in using this approach. If you fail to pick a profitable currency pair, then you will most likely lose a lot of money. Use this strategy with caution. Be sure to follow on the market and stay updated on the latest news that may be relevant to your investment/trade.

Strategy 16:Scaling out

If scaling in is about adding and having more open positions, scaling out is about lowering your exposure to risk by closing out some of your positions. Hence, this is the opposite of scaling in. Let us say that you are very confident about a certain trade and so you make a big investment into it. However, as time goes by, you realize that it is starting not to be as profitable as you have thought. This usually happens when a news piece that can have a negative impact on a trade gets featured. Suddenly, you start to feel less confident of your trade; however you still think that it can still be profitable. Now, since you find it hard to predict how the market will respond and are now quite unsure of the profitability of your position, you can start scaling out by closing some of your positions or lowering your invested amount in a trade. This way you can still profit if the market turns out to be favorable; however, in case that the market becomes unfavorable, then scaling out would be able to cut back your losses effectively.

So, how do you know when to scale in and when to scale out? This depends on how you think the market will move. If you predict that the market will move favorably, then scaling in would be the better option. However, if you become unsure of the profitability of your position, then scaling out would be the better option. In a volatile market where your position earns a profit but you are aware that it will soon take a downhill, scaling out will allow you to continuously take advantage of the current price movement with a much lower risk.

Strategy 17:Scaling in

Scaling in is where you enter a trade little by little or in pieces instead of putting everything in one position all at once. A trader who is looking to scale in may want to divide his position into quarters or in any way he deems best. Scaling in is an effective way to control your risk as you get to have a better understanding of how the market moves.

For example, if the total amount that you are willing to invest in a trade is $200, you divide it in half (or in quarters or in any way that you want) to start scaling in. Let us say that you open a position and invest $100, if the position turns out to be favorable, then you realize a profit. It is now up to you whether you still want to add the other $100. Now, let us assume that after adding the other $100, the price movement reverses and you start to lose the trade, since you have an initial investment at a much lower cost and has already profited, then you will be able to lower your total losses. Of course, the drawback here is that in the vent that the trade continues to be profitable, you will not earn as much as if you just invested the whole $200 at once on the first trade. Still, this strategy is worth learning since it effectively lowers your risk. As you may already know, being too aggressive is not a suggested approach as it can exhaust your funds quickly. To stay longer in the market and remain profitable, you need to control your risk and minimize your losses.

Strategy 18:Hedging

Simply put, hedging is a way to protect yourself against a big loss. Consider it as an insurance in case something unexpected happens that can adversely affect you as a trader. There are brokers that will allow you to hedge directly where you can purchase a currency pair and at the same time place place a trade to sell the said pair. Although you may not have a net profit while both trades are open, you can earn more without taking on addition risk if you observe proper timing. The way a hedge protects you is by allowing you to open an opposite trade while you are also trading the same currency pair. Of course, as a trader, you are free to just close your initial trade and then move to a new trade. A good thing about hedging is that you can save your trade and even make money if the market suddenly moves against your initial position. Now, in case the market reverses and takes a direction that is favorable to your first trade/position, then you can place a stop on the hedging trade or simply close it. This is the simplest way of hedging.

It is worth noting that hedging is not suggested tobe used by beginners. Its proper application requires adequate knowledge of the market, price swings, and proper timing.

Strategy 19:Swing trading

Swing trading is a long-term trading strategy. As a swing trader, you should expect to experience multiple price fluctuations. This is norm on the forex market, especially if you hold a position for a long period. A good thing about being a swing trader is that you can earn a high amount of profit by the time that you close your position. Another advantage of using this strategy is that you do not have to study the market every day. Although it is still advised that you at least check on the market on a daily basis. This is just to ensure that your position is not being compromised. From time to time, you at see that you are losing the trade, but do not panic. Again, you should expect for some price fluctuations to take place. The important thing is to be in a profitable position when you exit the trade. Hence, do not allow yourself to be affected by the day-to-day volatility of the forex market for such is bound to happen.

Of course, you cannot expect to make a profit simply by holding on to a particular position for a long term. It is still important for you to choose the right currency to invest in. How you pick a currency depends on you. You may use financial analysis, technical analysis, or any other approach that you prefer. Unlike momentum trading where you normally just aim for a small profit, swing trading usually brings a significant amount of profit since it has a much longer trading period. The drawback is that this is also the style of trading that can lead to a serious loss since it involves holding your position for a long time. Although swing traders usually ignore the day-to-day fluctuations in price even in the case of a loss, these fluctuations can easily pile of up over time and turn into a significant amount. This is also an excellent strategy to use for part-time traders as you do not have to follow the market regularly. Most swing traders only make a few trades in a month. The key is to focus on the quality of the trade than on quantity.

Strategy 20:Momentum trading

The key to this strategy is to identify strong price movements. The idea behind this strategy is that a strong price movement that is headed towards a particular direction is most likely going to continue for some more time. After all, the fluctuation caused by a strong price movement cannot be expected to counterbalance itself quickly. Momentum trading usually uses the same graphs and charts used in technical analysis since it deals directly with the price movements of a currency pair. Since momentum trading only aims to take advantage of the momentum of a strong price movement by following its direction, it is only suitable for short-term trading. This strategy is actually easy to use. You simply need to spot a strong price movement and take advantage of it before the trend changes.

Another important part of momentum trading is knowing when to close your position. It can sometimes be very tempting to hold your position and hope for the momentum to last longer. The problem is that by the time you realize that the momentum has already stopped, your profits might have already turned into losses. Therefore, in order to avoid this from happening, you should avoid getting greedy. The key is to exit the momentum trade even before it stops. Now, there is no hard and fast rule as to how you can determine up to how long a momentum trade is going to last. To be safe, just aim for a small profit and exit the position once you hit it. Do not forget that this strategy is about taking advantage of the momentum, which means that a strong price movement has already taken place, so do not hold on to the position for too long.

Strategy 21:Scalping

If you would rather have small but consistent profit, then you should learn scalping. Since the potential profit is small, your risk will also be small. Of course, the key to profit with this strategy is having multiple small profits. Therefore, as a scalper, you need to be patient and diligent at the same time. If you are the type of trader who only wants to profit a big amount quickly, then this is not for you. Basically, scalping is where you enter a position and then leave it the moment that you realize a profit. Hence, this strategy is perfect for day traders. An important element of scalping is identifying the currency pair to invest in. Some traders merely rely on the volatility that is inherent in the forex market. However, it is worth noting that merely relying on volatility is not good enough. Instead, you need to rely on the hard facts and actual details. Therefore, as a trader, you are expected to do as much research as possible to help you develop your own understanding of the market.

When you use scalping, you should keep a close eye on the market while your position is open. All you need is a small profit, and then you should close your position. It is an excellent short-term strategy. Another important element of scalping is to know when to close your position. It can be very tempting to continuously hold a position, especially when you are profiting from it. However, keep in mind that holding on to a position for a longer time also increases your risk. After all, the fact remains that no matter how profitable a position may be, the market can still suddenly fall at any time. When you use scalping, you should minimize your risk as much as possible. Do not worry; if your position is truly profitable, you can still get back to it. The important thing about scalping is to be able to profit a little by risking also a little. Do not be greedy. Scalping is effective, but it takes time and you will have to do it many times to earn a significant amount of profit.

A notable disadvantage of using scalping is that it requires a large deposit; otherwise, the profit that you will get per successful trade would be almost negligible. If you do not invest a big amount, then you would earn very little even after ten successful trades using scalping.

Strategy 22:Technical Analysis

If you are more of a visual person, then you might want to learn technical analysis. Most traders use this strategy due to its effectiveness and simplicity. If you think that fundamental analysis is too tiring, then technical analysis combines everything altogether that all that you need to do is to analyze graphs and charts. The concept behind this strategy is that all of the factors or elements that affect the different currencies have their final effect upon the price. Therefore, by simply analyzing the price movements of the different currencies as shown by the graphs, you get to deal with all the said elements. After all, regardless of what is happening in the world, the only thing that truly matters is how the prices of the currencies move in the market. If you are able to predict their movements, then you can easily take appropriate actions and earn a decent profit.

The key to technical analysis is to be able to read patterns. Yes, patterns do exist. In fact, if you allow a random generator to play for some time, it will also create some patterns. It is worth remembering that patterns come and go. Therefore, do not expect to see a pattern every time that you look at a graph. A common problem with traders who use technical analysis is that they force to see a pattern even when it does not really exist. Do not delude yourself. Keep in mind that you are not obliged to enter a trade. Therefore, only make a trade when you see a good opportunity to profit. Just because you have spent about an hour or two analyzing a pattern does not mean that you should make a decision to trade right away. When you use technical analysis, patience is an important virtue that you should learn. Now, in the event that you identify a pattern, then you should act quickly and take advantage of it.

Technical analysis is definitely one of the strategies that you should learn as a trader. It is also not uncommon to see traders who use this strategy with another strategy. Once you learn how to **read** graphs and charts, you will easily be able to draw information simply by looking at them. Hence, no matter what strategy you use, you can always use your skill in reading charts to help you come up with a better trading decision. Once again, the more information and understanding that you have about a particular currency or currencies, the more likely that you will be able to predict their movement. Needless to say, this kind of knowledge is something that you can turn into a profit.

Strategy 23: Fundamental Analysis

This analysis is sometimes referred to as the **lifeblood of investment** for good reasons. As its name suggests, fundamental analysis deals with the fundamentals or the basics. Take note that **basics** does not mean that it is composed of elements that are easy to understand. Rather, **basics** refer to the very foundation of things. In forex trading, this involves knowing and analyzing fundamental indicators to see if a particular currency is undervalued or overvalued relative to another currency. Fundamental analysis also analyzes the different factors or elements that affect the prices of the different currencies. An important part of fundamental analysis is to be updated in the news. In fact, some people refer to fundamental analysis as news analysis since this approach is primarily concerned about being updated on the news and analyzing it. When you apply fundamental analysis, the step is to be aware of the news that may have an effect upon the prices of different currencies, especially those that may affect the currencies that you want to trade. Keep in mind that there are many factors that can influence the price of a currency, such as the economy, technological developments, market acceptance and use, the level of competition, government relations and regulations, and businesses, among other things. So, for example, if you read in a newspaper that there is underemployment in the United States, and all other things being equal, then there is a good chance that the price of the U.S. dollar can decrease. Once you know this, then you can take appropriate actions to take advantage of it. You should also check the record of the currency inflows and outflows. This is published b the central bank. Of course, when you use fundamental analysis, you are expected to spend lots of time doing research and analysis.

As a professional trader, fundamental analysis should be a part of your life. When it come to the forex market, the amount and quality of information that you have play a crucial role since trading decisions are based on what you know about the market. Hence, the more that you understand the market, the more that you will be able to come up with a sound investment decision. Fundamental analysis is also a strategy that you can combine with other strategies, such as technical analysis. Keep in mind that knowing the basics is important. In fact, many of the changes that occur in the prices of different currencies can easily be explained just by understanding the basics or the fundamentals.

CHAPTER 10 :

CHARTING TOOLS FOR FOREX

Tools of trade

This is a term used to help a person decide the kind of property they should use to earn and make a living. According to bankruptcy law, the exemption for tools of the trade is usually determined by the state in the state exemption statutes. The exemption can also be determined by federal law in the federal bankruptcy exemptions. The period of time in which a person lived in a state before filing could also be a determinant of the exemption. Lawyers assist their clients to understand which properties are exempt and the exemptions apply.

Anything a person can prove they use as a tool for trade is marked as a separate exemption from assets they own. This means that a person can be allowed an exemption for households separately from assets they use to make a living. One person may provide their vehicle as a property they own while another may produce their vehicle as a taxi which earns him his daily bread.

Having the right tools for trading will guarantee success for anyone starting. An experienced trader may not really be concerned about the tools they use but for beginners, the tools count.

Examples of Tools Used For Trade.

Light speed financial broker – here a broker or a group of brokers breaks into different groups of specialization. The specialization is determined by the services they offer and the financial instrument used. The options for these brokers are Forex, stocks, long term investing and scalping brokers. Light speed brokers are very convenient for day time traders because of their direct accessibility and fast executions.

Trade ideas stock scanning software – after establishing a good broker, the next step is finding the stock to trade with. The ability to determine stocks before they make a big move is what determines a more profitable trader. Trade ideas software helps in stock scanning for volume spikes, HOD movers to establish the gainers and the losers and things like that. This is the best software there is that scans the market and finds the winning stocks.

signal charting – the third step is getting high-quality charts. The broker you chose makes come his standard charts. Those will work for you for some time until you decide to use ones that allow you to draw and write formulas. Signal allows one to run charts on 8 monitors without time delay. This is advantageous to people who like observing several stocks at once. it also allows installation of custom scripts. Custom scripts can be used as custom indicators for reversals and drawing support and resistance lines.

Breaking news provider – every morning, a trader should start by reviewing the market. After the review, you look at the catalyst to determine why stocks are moving higher. Reasons for the stocks could be moving up in consideration to the market, or a strong sector while other times it may be a unique catalyst like earnings. Breaking news provide the headlines for when the stocks are spiking.

TAS market profile – this software is best in helping make trade decisions. It has several tools in it. Among them is a TAS scanner which allows one to observe stocks moving at different timings with different levels of buying and selling.

Having the right tool may not guarantee success in the trading world but it will give the right directions that will help make trading easier. The right tool will also provide an advantage for a trader over other traders who do not have the tools. Indicators of Trade

This is a measure or gauge of trade that allows analyzing of prices and provides trade signals. Indicators provide trade signals that alert a trader when it is time to trade. Day trading indicators are not to be used as the only plan. They should be used along with a well laid out though to make it a useful trading tool. No matter the kind of trade one is involved in, having many trading indicators may bring inconsistency with trading decisions due to the complexities involved. Keeping it simple could simply be the trick to making clear and less stressful trading decisions.

Trading indicators should not, therefore, be taken as the only method relied on trading. However, using indicators alongside other trading variables may come in handy. Getting rid of the many indicators helps traders have a simplistic approach to the market.

Role of Technical Indicators

Get the direction trend

Determine the momentum or lack of momentum in the market

Determine if and if not the market is growing

Get the volume to determine how popular a market is with traders

Getting the same type of indicators that on the chart that give the same information is where the issue is. This is because you may give conflicting information or get more information than you may be stressful. The main shortcoming of most indicators is that since they are gotten from price, they delay the price. There are rules that one can use to determine useful indicators for day trading, swing trading, and position trading. This include among others:

Choosing one trend indicator such as moving average and one momentum trading indicator is the simplest rule.

Knowing well the perimeters you want to investigate before you decide on the trading indicators which you will use on your charts. Then know well the indicator you chose in terms of how it works, calculations it does and the effects it will bring for your trading decisions.

Indicators work only depending on how they are incorporated into the trading plan. Some indicators like MACD and CCI are best at calculating information. Others like alligator indicator are fast at showing a market that is trending and ranging. Other indicators will show directions and act as entry and exit signals of trade. The usage of a basic indicator along with a well laid out trading plan by back,forward and demo can you put you ahead of trade with many complicated indicators. Netpicks offers systems that test trade plans, prove trading systems and trading indicators. Threat of Optimization

There is a hindrance or barriers for when one is searching for trading indicators that work for one's style and trading plan. Most systems sell standard indicators that are fine-tuned to show successful results from the past. This is a disadvantage since it does not take into account the market changes. Using the standard settings for all indicators help avoid over-optimization trap which helps a trader not to focus on today's market progress and miss on the future.

Best Technical Trading Indicators

For day trading, a trader should test several indicators individually then later as a combination. One may end up with say 3-5 good ones that are evergreen and decide to switch off depending on the market at that particular day or the asset trading. Regardless of the type of trade, day, Forex or futures the idea is to keep it simple with the indicators. Use one indicator per category to avoid repeating the same thing and distraction.

Combining Indicators

Combining pairs of indicators on the price chart helps to identify points to initiate trade. A good example is a combination of RSI and moving average convergence which combined suggest and reinforce a trading signal. When choosing sets it's important to find one indicator considered a leading indicator and another that is a lagging indicator.

Leading indicators show signals before the forms for entering trade has been made. Lagging indicators on the other hand show signals after the formation have happened. Therefore lagging indicators can confirm leading indicators and help a trader from trading on wrong signals.

Choosing a combination of pairs that include indicators of different types instead of the same type is highly advisable. It does not make sense to observe a combination of the same type of indicators because they will still give the same information.

Multiple Indicators

Using multiple indicators boosts trading signals and may increase chances of telling out false signals.

Refining Indicators

It is important for a trader to take note and record the performance of the indicators they are using. Knowing the weaknesses of an indicator to determine if it gives a lot of false signals, if sometimes it fails to signal or if it signals too late or too early is essential. Knowing these things about the indicator will help determine what the indicator is best suited for. You may find that the indicator is suited for Forex instead of stocks while you thought it was just ineffective. This might help you decide if you want to trade the indicator for another or to just simply change how it's calculated. Doing this refining, will help an indicator work best for you, and also for you to find the best indicator for different types of trading.

Patterns of Trade

This is generally how trade takes place. It is the movement of price against a specific period of time. Patterns of trade are made of charts drawn in lines to connect proportional prices like the closing dates for a number of days.

Hammer Patterns

This is a reversal candlestick pattern that happens at the bottom of the depression. It is created when the open, high, and close prices are about the same price and a lower long shadow twice the length of the main body happens.

Even when a hammer pattern is a single candle, an observation of the surrounding candles within that single stick is needed to confirm if it is indeed a hammer candlestick pattern.

Verification Signals

When the candle has a long lower shadow, there is a high chance of price reversal. When there is a lot of trade volume the day the hammer forms, it probably means a blow off in the trade.

When the candle has a gap from the previous day closing price, it means that a strong reversal is expected to happen because the price opened higher a day after the hammer.

A green candle will show the sign of a bull while a red sign will show the sign of a bear.

The Inverted Hammer Pattern

This candlestick is formed after depression and is a sign of a trend reversal. It looks like the reverse of a hammer candlestick pattern and its formation indicates an uptrend called a shooting star. If there is a downtrend and an inverted hammer with the sign of a bull is formed, it means that the prices delayed the upward move by a high increase during the day. Then the sellers made the prices push back near the open. Prices having increased show the bulls trying to overpower the bears. The next day determines if the prices go higher or lower and their observation is very important.

The bullish pattern is a continuous pattern that represents a fall in the market after a strong unexpected move. The bullish pattern does not necessarily require the use of an indicator because it is itself a price action. The bullish flag pattern is a strong technical pattern in that it has the ability to form in the shortest time frame of a minute up to a whole monthly chart. This pattern is constructed in two sections; the first is a powerful sustained rally while the other one is that, it has a tight range that is contained in two parallel lines.

There has been an immense growth in the global economy over the years. This has resulted in a change in the pattern trade. The changes include deindustrialization, the participation of communist countries and the emergence of India and China. Although growth has been affected by short term changes due to the economic cycle, the value of trade has immensely improved. Globalization is taking over. Trade openness has also increased in most countries as an effect of globalization.

UNDERSTANDING CHART

We have been talking about how you should refer to charts when you are conducting your Forex transactions. But that begs the question, is there Forex software that will meet your needs and at the same time provide you with tons of features?

The satisfying answer is that there is!

That software is TradingView.

Let's start with a brief summary of what TradingView is all about.

So what exactly is the TradingView?

It is convenient charting software that also provides traders with the ability to network on the platform. TradingView is ideal for all kinds of trades, whether they are beginners or veterans. It is meant to provide you with a visual representation your trading (which is what we want after all) and supplements that view with tons of information about the trade.

Here are some of the cool features of the software:

Depending on how you would like to approach your trade, you can create simple charts or complex dynamic and multi-layered charts to track a plethora of markets. Additionally, if you feel like it, you can even create your own charts on the platform.

The software comes with different kinds of alerts that you can modify on the platform. Based on what kind of information you require urgent updates about, you can adjust up to 12 different notification settings.

For those who have honed their skills in charting software, TradingView also provides the feature of "Pine Script". What this script allows you to do is create your indicators and charts.

The platform also gives you access to over 50 exchanges around the world, enough to fulfill all your trading needs.

Finally, to add the cherry on the cake, TradingView provides a lot of educational materials. They have everything from videos to podcasts to articles giving you details on how you can trade and how you can manage finances, to how you should be looking at the various charts. Simply put, you have all the information you need to get started on the platform and become acclimated to the Forex world.

You can sign up for a free account, but it is not necessary to view some of the information on the platform. If you would like to simply make a quick reference, then head over to TradingView and you will spot a ticker on the top of the website giving you updates about the popular currency pairs.

MOBILE CHARTING PLATFORMS

Today's world is all about going mobile. If you have a business, it has become vital to target mobile users. It is for this reason that platforms such as Facebook, Google, YouTube, and Instagram all have special marketing campaigns that target mobile users.

In the same way, there are numerous mobile versions of charting platforms that you can access from anywhere in the world, as long as you are connected to a network.

But out of all the platforms available to you, which ones are actually worth looking into? Here are the ones you should consider if you are going to work on charts.

TD Ameritrade

TD Ameritrade makes a comeback! Earlier, we talked about the desktop version of the app. Here, we are going to focus on the mobile version. Not only is the app one of the most established and trusted platforms in the U.S., but it is also regulated (as we have seen before). The information on the app is presented in a clear manner. TD Ameritrade also focuses on other products such as futures, stocks, and options.

Trade Interceptor

Trade Interceptor is mainly made for advanced users. Though it does have a friendly interface and numerous educational materials to use, it is targeted to those who have more experience dealing with the Forex market. Its main charm is the fact that it provides access to a myriad of indicators that you can use for your trades. The app is also powered by the cloud network, allowing you to transfer your profile to any device. You can even play around with a trading simulator, designed to try out your strategies before you get down to working on real trades.

Forex Time FXTM

What does Forex Time FXTM have in its favor that most other platforms do not? It has a degree of trustworthiness. After all, it has been used in nearly 180 countries and regulated in numerous regions as well. The platform is designed to work for both beginners, as the app itself is fairly easy to use, and for professionals, as it gives access to advanced features and educational materials. It also offers speedy functionalities and is able to make trades with just a percentage of a second difference between the time you execute and the time the order has been confirmed.

Netdania

One of the highlights of this app is that it provides you with trading strategies and ideas. The creators of the app have marketed the platform as a "personal trading assistant" and in many ways, it does function that way. For example, the app actually gives you a notification to let you know when the right time to go long or go short is. While doing this, it accumulates real-time news and economic information from around the world. Through social networking features, it shares strategies between various traders. This means that you can use the app to copy someone else's trading techniques if they have been successful.

As the app is connected to a cloud platform, you can easily share your info and details between multiple devices. Meaning that if you lose your mobile device, you can always download the app on another phone and get your data back.

CHAPTER 11:

BEST FOREX TRADING STOP LOSS STRATEGIES

HOW DO YOU SET STOP LOSS IN FOREX TRADING?

This is the most common problem among marketers. How to adjust the stop loss to protect its position but not to be stopped too soon? The benefit is that it's easier to set loss thresholds with Fibonacci business tools. In this segment, we will discuss more the basics of stop-loss setup and more advanced tips.

Should you use stop-loss orders?

Lately, I have read a few opinions that the use of stop loss is bad. I will not beat everyone here. If a professional trader finds that losses are not needed, then it's up to you. If he makes money, that's fine. But if you are a new investor and have trouble closing a successful year, you should use the Stop Loss method.

Let's say clearly and loudly: the losses are not perfect. It's not something that makes you rich or profitable. Something is not 100% accurate. You adjust your stop loss, and your stop loss is as good as the good trader you are.

Why stop loss are great?

Stop losses are great because they protect you from your network and your impulsive decisions. Can you remember the number of times you have waited too long to close the losing trade? You were hoping it was just a correction and the buyers will come back in a moment.

Emotions are your worst advisor. You can not disable them completely, but you can work by minimizing their impact on your negotiations. Stopping the loss order is one of the tools that can help you achieve this goal.

The idea of stop loss

The idea of putting a good stop loss down is to help you limit your losses and prevent emotions from taking control of your decisions. In this way, you can have three missed offers as a result, but the loss of these three offers will not be so serious. The next exchange can be much more lucrative.

Let's take a look at the example.

John wants to purchase 200 shares of YYY Company for $ 12. He is willing to risk $ 1.2 per share. He has a good impression on this company, and his business plan gives him the green light. He bought it, and two days later it was banned. His loss was 1.2 x 200 shares = $ 240.

The next day, he decides to embark on another job. There was a leak in the VVV table. He buys 80 shares at $ 20 and sets his direct deficit at $ 1.5. At first, it sounds good, but suddenly there is a rumor about YYY's problems, and the actions start to fall. He was prevented. Your loss is 1.5 x $ 80 shares = $ 120.

He is not happy, but he is looking for other opportunities. He has few possible candidates but has decided to wait for a new confirmation of his bargaining plan. A few days later, there is a confirmation signal on the HHH company charter. He purchases 50 shares for $ 42 and sets his share at $ 38.5. Not much next action days, but eventually, the stock starts to increase. In the coming weeks, HHH will reach $ 52, and John decides to close the deal because there is a strong resistance close to this level. He closed the position at $ 52 and his profit was 50 shares x ($ 52 - $ 42) = $ 500.

In the previous two transactions, he lost $ 360, so his profit is $ 500 - $ 360 = $ 140. Okay, it's not achieved, but it's not that bad. But if the losses of previous trades were greater? So, he would always try to get his money back.

The example is simple, but I hope you have the main idea. It's a life of investors. You will be arrested. Their goal is to seek lucrative contracts and, through them, to earn money and cover their losses.

Risk / Ratio reward

There is a very big goal of maintaining your risk/return ratio in ratios of 1: 2 or even 1: 3. This means that the trader is willing to risk, for example, $ 2 per share and hope to win $ 4 per share. (1: 2) or 6% (1: 3).

If the risk/return ratio is about 1: 1, they do not go into a business because they are not worth that risk.

The risk/reward description is a good topic for another book. For now, let's stay on the risk part. Experienced traders are looking for good opportunities to know where to stop. They do not go into a negotiation and then ask, "Hmmm, maybe here's a good place to stop the loss." They know it fundamentally when they are considering trading because they are looking for a good risk/return ratio. Keep this in mind.

When to set stop losses

The best practice is to set the stop loss when you place the order. You must know in advance where you want to define your stop loss. When you place your order, you set the Stop Loss program on the right path. Why Because then you will probably hesitate to put SL. You can also put it in the wrong place because of emotions.

Below are the Forex trading stop loss strategies:

Placing a Stop Loss below the Last Low

You can still place a stop loss at the last significant low when you are in a long position. When the trend is stable, you should make some profit. But when the trend is weak, you'll be stopped out. That is okay because the price will go lower than the stop loss. The same applies in a downtrend. You could be looking forward to placing your stop loss above the last high.

Set Stop-Loss in a Downtrend

In case the downtrend goes past the previous high, then buyers should attempt to take over the control. You don't want to run short in this case, so you should close your position and look for other opportunities.

Increasing the Stop Loss

Many forex traders don't like to use this technique, yet it is the best. First, you place your stop loss once you open a trade. There are times when you'll get stopped fast, but the trade should continue. However, the most critical point comes when you have a profitable trade position. Can it change and shake your stop loss?

When faced with this situation, increase your stop loss to the entry point. That means if the price goes against your position, you won't lose a single dollar. That leads to another interesting question. When is the right time to increase the stop loss? Well, don't do it immediately when you make a profit. Wait for some time and monitor the trade. You need to master how to play around with your system but in a smart way.

Sometimes, the price may continue to rise when you expect it to drop. In this case, continue to increase your stop loss even further. By increasing your stop loss, you will be protecting your profit. When the price doesn't reach your target, close the trade with the profit that you have made. This is an example of trailing stop loss because the stop loss rises as the price increases. There are other methods that you can use to trail stop loss. That is for you to find out. Remember, it is from trying out that you find the best one to use.

The 1% Rule

Some traders use the 2% rule. The 1% rule requires traders to risk only 1% of their trading capital on any single trading position. However, because of small capital, many traders don't follow this rule. The best thing about this rule is that even when you have ten losing trades, you'll still retain a good percentage of your money. So you can see why you should train yourself to follow the 1% rule. Whether you have $100 in your account or more than $100, learn to use this rule if you don't want to lose all your money. Forex trading can be risky, especially when the market is volatile. Nobody will force you to use this rule, but you should make it a habit of using it in any trade that you open.

Money management tips

Is there a secret to success in forex trading? No. But there are a few things that all successful traders do, and are no secret. You merely have to be smart with money management.

Money management is not a new term in forex. It is just the knowledge and skill you use to manage your Forex trading account. That is the secret to a long successful trading career. Although many traders forget to use it, this section outlines ground rules that you can follow to control your account effectively.

Don't be carried away with making big money. This may cause you to lose a lot of money. There is no easy money in forex trading. To be successful in trading, you must learn to be patient and learn to trade small. Not all trades will give you profits. That is why you should plan on losses.

Another thing that you must do is to risk a small percent of your money on each trade. By doing this, you will reduce the risk of losing all your money. You can risk either 1% or 2% of your money. However, experienced traders go as high as 5%, but not more than that. Remember. It is easy to lose money in forex, but hard to regain.

Use Limit Orders

Successful traders know how to use a stop loss. Stop loss will control how much profit you make. A stop loss order will protect your investment and allow you to make small gains.

The Size of Your Trades

Traders are advised to open small trading positions. One of the reasons for this is because when you have a losing trade, you can decide to open another reverse trade position to compensate your losses.

Learn To Practice with Virtual Money

There is a good reason why the virtual method of trading was invented. Don't ignore it. Test all your trading strategies with virtual money before you start to trade on a real trading account. When you switch to actual trading, don't stop to use a virtual account when you want to test a new strategy. Don't risk your money on a real account that may cause you to lose all your money.

Always Automate Your Trading

It is appropriate that you should always try your best to automate your trading platform. I have already talked about the importance of emotional control. However, you can minimize the role of emotions by automating your trading choices as well as your trade behaviors. All you need is to ensure that your trading system produces similar responses to trading scenarios and similar situations that you would have provided.

Don't Give Up

Only risk what you can afford to lose. Forex trading requires commitment, determination, and persistence. You will not just wake up and become a trading genius within a day. Forex requires that you be patient and learn with time. Before giving up, ripen your skills and develop your talents as long as there is no pain in the learning process and the risks involved will not derail your future and life plans.

Always Keep A Printed Record

When I began doing Forex trading, I always printed all the trade charts. Printed records provided me with a great learning tool. I would, therefore, advise you as a beginner to always print out the charts and then list all the reasons as to why you are doing the trade. List the fundamental reasons you feel swayed your decisions. In your printed chart, mark your entry and exit points. Also ensure that on the chart, you include emotional reasons for taking the actions you took. For instance, if you were anxious, panicked or you were just greedy, put them all there. By objectifying your trades, you will be able to develop strong mental controls as well as discipline that will guide you in executing trade in accordance with your system and not your emotions of personal habits.

Be Consistent With Doing Weekend Analysis

The Forex markets are usually closed on the weekends. When closed, take your time to have a deep study on the weekly charts so as to identify the patterns or news that can have effects on your trade. For instance, you may notice that a particular trade pattern is indicating a double top but the new and pundits, on the other hand, are making suggestions that there will be a reversal in the market. In the real sense, this kind of reflexivity could only be there to promote some pattern prompting the pundits to reinforce it. Therefore, be patient and according to your best plan, set up your things and follow your objectives.

Be Motivated By Positive Feedback Loops

By having trade plans that are well executed, you definitely will create a positive feedback loop pattern. As always, success breeds success. You will feel confident when the trade is profitable. Furthermore, take losses but ensure that they are small according to your trade plan. This will help you build a positive feedback loop.

Focus On Minimizing Losses

Once you have made the decision to invest in Forex trade and you have funded your account, but it clearly in your mind that your money is at risk. Therefore,avoid making this trading money to be money used for your regular living expenses but rather look at it as vacation money. Develop an attitude in you that directs you towards trading. With this attitude, you will be psychologically prepared to accept small losses. This is a basic step in risk management. A trader who gives their focus on trade and accepts small losses are more successful than those who focus on constantly counting their equity. To be a professional trader, you must recognize the available markets. However, in order to recognize the markets, begin by first recognizing yourself. Assess yourself and be aware of your capital allocation for Forex as well as your tolerance to risks. Just ensure that they are not lacking or excessive. You have to master your financial goals and understand why you are engaging Forex trading.

Always Begin With Small Sums

The best tip for any Forex trader wishing to be a professional trader is by beginning with a small account and then increase the size of your account through profits. Don't start by investing heavily. Don't be confused by the idea that larger accounts will lead you to greater profits. It is perfect when you are able to increase your account size through trading choices. Otherwise, I don't see the need of you pumping money to an account that will only lead you to strain your finances and emotions.

Be Sure To Calculate Your Expectancy

Basically, expectancy will help you to determine your system's reliability. It is advised that as a trader, you should try to roll back and check your trade history. From here, get a measurement of your winning trades and losing trades. Try to compare the profitability of your winning trades versus the loss of the losing trades. For instance, you can have a look at the last ten trades you have made. Suppose you have not yet made any actual trades, I advise that you go back on your chart. Try to check whether the trading activities would have resulted in losses or profits. Now proceed to total the winning trades found and then divide this total wins. The below formula will guide you;

Expectancy (E) = [1 + (L/ W)] × P – 1

Where we have W and L as the average of the winning trade and losing trade respectively and P being the winning ratio percentage

Case Example

Having made ten trades, out of these ten, you have won 7 and lost 3, the percentage win ratio is [(10-3)/ 10] which is equivalent to 7/ 10 (70%). Suppose that these seven trades earned you $ 4,200, your average win will be ($ 4,200/ 7) = $ 600. Again suppose your losses summed to $ 1,500, the average loss in the ten trades made will be [$ 1,500/ (10-7)] = $ 500. Now apply the use the formula we used to get the expectancy.

E = [1 + (600/ 500)] x 0.7 - 1

E = [1 + 1.2] x 0.7 - 1

E = [2.2] x 0.7 -1

E = 1.54 - 1

E = 54%

This means that your system is likely to give you a positive 54% expectancy and your expected return will be about 50 cents per dollar you invest.

Study the Forex Market and Its Fundamentals

Having a deep understanding of the fundamentals of Forex market and the technical factors affecting the price action is of great importance. Without a reasonable understanding of the Forex market, you are likely to be affected by negatively. However, don't be afraid of the consequences of erroneous application or the consequences of failing to understand the technical or fundamental studies. Learning is a gradual step and as we make errors, we get to learn more. You must have proper money management skills as well as emotional skills as these play important role in the analysis. It is also appropriate that once you make profits, learn how to protect them. I suggest that if you have no skills in money management, learn. Money management will teach you how to minimize your losses and maximize your profits. I prefer that you develop a bible of money management and put it as trading library's centerpiece. This will guide you on ways of ensuring that you don't gamble with the profits you have earned hardly as well as cut your losses short.

Clearly Determine Your Entry and Exit Points

Often many beginners are usually confused by when going through the information presented in the charts in the different timeframes. This is due to the fact that most of the times the information presented in these charts are so conflicting. There are times when what is shown on the weekly chart as the buying opportunity can be shown up on the intraday chart as a sell signal. It is advised that as a Forex beginner, if you have chosen to shift your trading to a daily chart say from a weekly chart, ensure that you synchronize these two charts. What I mean is that, suppose your weekly chart gives a buy signal, be patient for the release of a daily chart to confirm a similar signal. Just be sure to keep your timing in sync.

Before Moving to Multiple Currency Pair, Focus More on One Currency Pair

By now, I believe that you have noted that the Forex trade world is a complicated world. This is probably attributed to the mixed-up nature of the currency market,the different goals different participants have and the wide and diverse characters. Unless you are a genius, it will be very difficult to understand all the financial and economic activities going around the world. Therefore, to be a successful Forex trader, it is important that you try to stick your Forex trade activities the currency pairs you are familiar with and have a good understanding of. It is an even greater advantage if you start with your nation's currency. However, if this is not what you want, I prefer that you chose the widely and most liquid traded currency pairs.

Choosing Of A Broker And A Trading Platform

It is appropriate that you chose a reputable broker. I advise that as a beginner, start by taking a considerable amount of time to do deep research on the differences between the available brokers. Try to understand the different policies that each broker has as well as how each of these brokers goes about making a market. You have to understand that doing trade in the over-the-counter market differs from exchange driven market. Again, I advise that you be sure of the trading platform your broker is using so as to know the suitable analysis that will fit you. For instance, if you trade by analyzing Fibonacci numbers, just ensure that the platform your broker is using also supports the drawing of Fibonacci lines. Try to understand good brokers with poor trading platforms, poor brokers with good trading platforms and good brokers with good trading platforms. Ensure that you choose a good broker with a good trading platform.

CHAPTER 12:

DEVELOPING YOUR OWN
TRADING PLAN

You now have the fundamental principles of Forex trading under your belt and you are aware what you are trading in and why. So how do you translate that into a practical application?

Every successful trader enters the marketplace with a clear plan in their mind and the reason they can then describe themselves as successful is because they follow it dutifully and religiously.

Now, while it's true that you can find software out there that will make those decisions for you, I strongly recommend that you avoid the temptation. Much as with those crash diets that never help lose more than a couple of pounds and the wonder medicines that do little else than taste unpleasant, those software programs tend to be snake oil. After all, if they really did work, everyone would be using them and everyone would be millionaires.

Instead, you're going to have to create your own plan and then rely on your hard work to research the markets, your intuition and your ability to assess risk to provide the rest.

To get started is relatively simple. You will need to provide yourself the answer to two questions:

What is the maximum loss you are prepared to make on a single position? (In percentage terms.)

What will be your stop loss position on your trades?

Every trader needs to know the answer to those questions, although everything else is fluid and personal. Your ability to analyze the market, the time of day you trade, your capital and risk ability – these things are all distinctly personal, which means there is no possible way to develop a plan that works for absolutely everybody.

Not to mention that the same strategy won't necessarily work in every market and on every trade or with every currency pair. You will need to develop a fluid mindset that can adapt your plan accordingly to the realities of the market.

So, with that in mind, how do you develop your personal strategy? Start with the two questions above, as these are designed to make sure that the capital in your trading account remains intact. Answer those questions with a mind to your trading account and to how much you can afford to lose before you no longer have the capital to continue trading. Your answers are the only ones to which you must adhere religiously, come what may. Consider your capital to be your prize possession and worthy of protection at all times.

A quick example to show you how those questions then apply to an actual trade. Let's assume that you've decided that your maximum risk on a trade is going to be $45, which equates to 2 percent of your capital (I would recommend never going above 5 percent), and that you've decided your stop loss position will represent three times the average pip movement of that currency pair.

Now let's assume you're looking at a trade that moves on average five pips within your chosen timeframe. You would therefore have a stop loss position of 15 pips. If you divide the maximum loss you're prepared to make by the number of pips, you get the number 3, which translates to $3 per pip.

So what does that mean? It means that you want a contract that balances out at $3 per pip.

You can, of course, then play with your equation. For example, if you enter into a contract with less risk than you're prepared to take, you can then increase your position later if your predictions bear out, adding more contracts until you reach that $45 maximum. Don't forget that the answer to these questions represents the maximum risk you're prepared to take, so you don't actually have to meet those numbers exactly as long as you don't exceed them.

Having a strong trading plan is an important part of successfully trading on the Forex market. Even the experts develop one, so it is important that as a beginner, you do too. In this chapter, you are going to learn about why you need a roadmap and how you can develop one.

What Is a Trading Plan?

Developing a trading plan allows you to define a goal and create a system for you to work towards that goal through your trades. Due to the volatility of the market, you cannot create a finite blueprint for your trading plan. However, you can create a general strategy and goals for you to work with. There are certain rules and elements to consider when you are developing your plan to ensure that you have one that is strong and will serve you for the best.

Who Needs One?

It is important that anyone who is doing trading on the Forex market, or anywhere else for that matter, to have a strong trading plan. This allows them the opportunity to reap in all of the benefits of having a trading plan from risk management to learning discipline in your trades. Even experts develop plans before entering the Forex market, so it is imperative that as a beginner, you also develop a plan.

Why Do You Need a Trading Plan?

There are a number of benefits to having a trading plan when you are getting involved in the Forex market. For one, it is great for you to minimize your risk due to your ability to have a plan for what you will do in certain scenarios. You can also use it to establish your exit strategies beforehand so that you know when you are going to exit if necessary. Having a plan also allows you to stay focused on your goal and make large strides towards that goal, so you can stay on par for your goals with your trading decisions. Another reason why having a plan is important is because it allows you to ensure that you are constantly evaluating your trades to ensure that your money is working well for you and that you are making strong decisions. If you find that your trades aren't having high enough yields or are too risky, you can reevaluate your plan and fix your strategy for a better outcome.

General Planning Rules

There are a few plans when you are preparing to trade on the market. There are no blueprints, though there are some considerations you need to think about when you are developing the plan. The following four "rules" are important when you are in the process of creating your trading plan, to ensure that you have the best results. Write down your goals all the time. If you make any changes, write that down as well. You will want to write down virtually every single part of your plan. This way, you can ensure that your thoughts are organized and your plan is solid. It also helps you stay focused on your goals and work towards them with every move you make. Make sure that in addition to writing out your plans, you record your progress as well. This allows you to see how your plan has worked, and to learn from previous trades that you have made as well so that you can continue to learn and make better decisions. This process will give you a better opportunity to improve your trading strategies and ensure that you recall which markets you have been exposed to.

Aside from writing everything down, you must control your finances. It is important that you manage your money properly in order to ensure that you are staying on top of everything to prevent yourself from investing too much into the market. You want to make sure that you are managing your risk and exposure and staying on top of how much you are making and losing in the grand scheme of things.

The best way to keep track of everything is to have a trading journal that allows you to keep track of your plan and all of the moves you make. It also allows you to keep track of your finances to ensure that you are making wise decisions and not investing too much or losing too much in certain moves.

Creating Your Plan

Before you create a plan, you need to ask yourself some questions. You should write these questions down in your trading journal to ensure that you are focused on what your goal is and that your plan aligns with the answers you have for the following questions.

Why do you want to trade with Forex?

What is your opinion on risk?

What is the amount of time you're willing to invest in trades?

How much do you know about trading already?

Identifying the answers to these questions is the best way to discover what your goals are with trading and how you position yourself in the market on trades that you will make.

You need to answer these questions before you start creating your plan, as they are the basis for the plans that you make.

Once you answer those four primary questions, there are more you will want to consider. The answer to these will be exactly what you need to know in order to create your specific plan and move forward with it. Your answers don't need to be deep and thoughtful, but they do need to be answered clearly.

Where are you right now, financially? Have you had any involvement in the market yet? If so, what is your involvement?

At this time, what type of trader are you? What are your thoughts on trading and risk?

Based on your level of knowledge right now, how confident do you feel in trading? What is the amount of capital you have to start your trading with?

What are your financial goals with your trading?

How long do you want to be trading for in order to reach that goal?

What is the success going to look like?

Answering these questions gives you a firm guideline of where you want to go and what you want to do with your trading. If you go in saying "I want to make a lot of money" but never define what "a lot" is, you are not going to be able to identify when you get there. You will also not know how to identify if you have been losing too much money. The market is something that you enter for specific purposes, as that is what will assist you in making the money you desire. You don't necessarily need to have a purpose such as retirement or education funds, but having a goal of what you want and a timeframe of when you want to achieve it will significantly assist you in mastering it and making as much as you desire.

Taking your trading to next level: develop your own trading rules

Having trading rules and following them with discipline is probably the last of essential things that you should have in your trading toolkit. You cannot expect to drift as a ship without direction in the market. You have to know what you are doing and why you are doing it. Otherwise, you will be eaten by the market. Forex is a zero sum game. In order for you to win, somebody has to lose. You can switch the parts. In order for somebody to win, you have to lose. You decide which part you want to take. If you want to be a winner you must have your own trading rules. Let's briefly look at them. Some of them you have heard as they have become slogans, others might be new to you. Anyway, you will surely need them.

Cut your losses short

Newbies hardly ever do that. They keep on expecting that the trade will come back and they will close it with a profit. It often happens, but when it doesn't they can lose half of their account or even all of it. Do not give in to wishful thinking. Cut your losses when they are still small. If your trade is going against you, it means something is not as you have planned and expected and the smartest thing to do is to get out of the market as fast as you can. Do not risk more than 2 percent of your account on any trade.

Let your profits run

Newbies do just the opposite. They let their losses run and cut their profits short. That's why they end up losing it all. The only way you can increase your trading account is by having bigger profits and smaller losses. If you make 100 pips and lose 200 you will soon be finished as a trader. Therefore, you have to make at least double of what you lose in order to be ahead. Trading is not easy and if you take a few pips and run, but let your losses to grow to hundreds of pips you will be finished sooner rather than later. Smart traders let their profits run. They catch a trend and they keep their positions till they outgrow their losses by three, four or even ten times. This is how money can be made in currencies.

Increase your exposure when you are doing well and reduce it when you fail

If you are doing well, you are in touch with the market and can take more risk, or simply open more positions in the direction of the market. This increases your chances to make bigger profits. On the other hand, you have to decrease your exposure to market if you are not doing that well. Trade less, when you have a number of losing trades. You need to have a fresh head, stable emotions and be disciplined when you take a trade. When you feel exhausted or you do not know where the market is going, just don't do anything. You don't have to trade. You have to use opportunities that you see, not the ones you don't see. Loses may force you in a psychological state where you want to recoup losses at any cost. Don't do that. This is a sure way to failure. Stop; let your head cool and only then trade.

Do not overtrade, select your trades

Overtrading is a common "disease" among new traders. They feel they need to be in the market all the time, because they are afraid of missing good trades. The fact is that they pick up a lot of bad trades, which far outweigh the good ones and this leads to never ending losses. If you want to be a good trader who makes money consistently you have to be very selective. Picking random trades will result in mediocre at best and at big losses in most cases.

Don't fight a trend

"Trend is your friend" is an old slogan that most professional Forex traders use. They want to trade in the direction of the prevailing trend and never against it. Money is made when you go with the market flow, not in the opposite direction. Newbies often rely on various indicators that tell them market is overbought or oversold and they start fighting a trend. The fact is that when trends start markets can stay in overbought or oversold territory for a long time. So, do not rely on those indicators and don't fight direction. Better, follow it. Trend trading is by far the easiest and most profitable trading system. Use it to make money.

Be aware of fundamental news releases

A single macroeconomic news release can cause a currency pair to move hundreds of pips in a matter of a few seconds. You do not want to have an open position that goes against you during those market events. Lots of pros simply close their positions before such important news releases as: interest rate decision, Non Farm Payrolls, CPI, General Domestic Product and a few more. Before a week starts, always look at Economic calendar to see which pieces of news are coming that week and do not trade during those events, only after market calms down and volatility comes back to normal levels.

Understand that market discounts information

Traders know that market participants always look forward. They expect things to happen. Therefore, when some piece of information comes out, it has already been priced in by market participant and market may go in the opposite direction that it is supposed to. Let's say market expects that FED will raise interest rates in half a year's time and the ECB will keep them the same. Now, this expectation pushes eur/usd down till finally the FED starts raising rates. When the news is finally released that interest rates have been increased the market will most likely sell off US dollar as it has already priced in this information.

Have a trading diary

You need to learn from your good and bad trades. Traders who don't learn become losers, because they keep on repeating the same mistakes and those finally cause them to lose everything. You need to monitor your trades, post a chart in your diary with an explanation why you opened a trade. Have some description or explanation as to what motivated you to take that trade. Did you follow your trading rules or you went against them? If it did not work, maybe you can find out why it happened. Have this practice every day and if you do not trade that often, at least once a week. You will see that with time you will make fewer mistakes and take a lot more better trades.

Be a learner

Be a learner. Read books about financial markets, various trading strategies, especially the materials that were published by successful traders. If you learn from them you will become a good trader much faster than you would if you did that all by yourself. You need to understand how good traders think, how they motivate themselves, how they analyze markets and etc. You can model them and eventually join the ranks of those who make consistent money in currencies.

CHAPTER 13:

CHOOSING YOUR TRADING STYLE

Before getting involved in trading actively forex market, take a step back, and think about how you want to approach the market. There is much more to currency trading than it seems, and we believe that the trading style you pick is one of the most important determinants of the overall success of trading.

Taking the emotion out of trading

So, how do you get the thrill of trading? The answer is simple: you can not. As far as your heart beats and your synapses fly away, the emotions will flow. And, to be honest, the high emotional levels of business are one of the reasons people get attracted to it in the first place. There is no hurry to doing business successfully and withdrawing money from the market. So accept that you will experience quite intense emotions during the negotiation.

The long answer is that because you can not block emotions, the best you hope to achieve is to understand where the emotions come from, recognize them when they hit, and limit the impact on your negotiations. It's very easy to say, but bear in mind some of the following to keep your emotions under control:

Concentrate on pips, not on dollars and cents. Do not

be distracted by the exact amount of money earned or lost in the exchange. Instead, focus on where the prices are and how they behave. The market has no idea how big your business is and how much you win or lose, but you know where the present price is.

It's not about being wrong or right; It's about making money. The market does not care whether you are right or wrong, and you should not either. The only real method used to measure a company's success is in dollars and cents.

You will lose in a reasonable number of transactions. No operator is always right. Taking losses is as routine as making profits. You can always succeed over time with a solid risk management plan.

Developing a disciplined trading plan

Whatever trading style you decide to adopt, you need an organized trading plan, or it does not go very far. The difference between losing cash and making cash in the foreign exchange market can be as simple as trading without a plan or trading with it. A trading plan is a prepared approach to execute a trading strategy that you have developed based on your analysis and market outlook.

Here are the main elements of any business plan:

Determine the size of the position: what is the size of your position for each trading strategy? The size of the position is half the equation to determine how much money is involved in each transaction.

Decide where to get into the position: where exactly are you going to try to open the desired position?

Setting Stop Loss and Take Profit Levels: Where exactly will you leave the position if it is a winning position (make a profit) and if it is a stop position? The stop-loss and take-profit levels are the second half of the equation that determines how much money is involved in each transaction.

That's it - just three simple components. But it's amazing how many new and seasoned traders open positions without ever thinking fully about their game plan. Of course, there are several tricky points to consider when developing a trading plan. But for the moment, we just want to get back to the point where negotiating without an organized plan is like flying a plane blindfolded - you can take off, but how are you going to land?

And regardless of how good your trading plan is, it will not work if you do not follow it. Sometimes, emotions arise and distract traders from their trading plans. Other times, unexpected news or a price movement forces traders to abandon their trading strategy halfway, or in the middle of trading , as the case may be. Anyway, when that happens, it's the same as never having a business plan in the first place.

Developing a market plan and sticking to it are the two main ingredients of corporate discipline. If we name the trait that defines successful traders, it would not be technical analysis skills, instinct, or aggression - although they are all important. No, it would be a commercial discipline. Traders who follow a disciplined approach are those who survive year after year and cycle aftermarket. They can even make mistakes more often and continue to make money because they follow a disciplined approach.

Carry trade strategies

So, let me clarify: you may be thinking: all I have to do is buy the most profitable currency / sell the worst-performing currency, sit down, earn the carry, and to watch the spot price rise? What is the question?

The problem is that the negative volatility of spot prices can quickly erase any gain in the carry trade differential. The risk can be exacerbated by the over-positioning of the market in favor of the carry trade, which means that they carry trade has become so popular that everyone gets into it.

When is a trend not a trend?

When it's a trading range, a range or market-related to a range is a market that remains confined to a relatively narrow price range.

Despite all the hype that trends have in various market publications, the reality is that most markets do not tend to be over a third of the time. The rest of the time, they jump at intervals, consolidate, and exchange laterally.

When short-term traders seek to take advantage of the routine noise of small price movements, almost disregarding the general direction of the market, medium-term transactions seek to gain the right direction and benefit from more favorable exchange rate movements. Important.

Almost as many currency investors fall into the medium-term category (sometimes called momentum trading and swing trading) as in the short-term category. Medium-term trading needs many of the same skills as short-term trading, particularly with respect to entry / exit positions, but it also requires a broader perspective, a greater analysis effort, and a lot more patience.

Capturing intraday price movements for maximum effect

The benefit of medium-term trading is to determine where a currency pair is likely to move in the next hours or days and developing a trading strategy to exploit that vision. Medium-term traders usually follow one of the following general approaches, with plenty of room to combine strategies:

Trading a View: Have a basic opinion about how a currency pair will likely evolve. The display operations are generally based on prevailing market themes, such as interest rate expectations or economic growth trends. Display traders must always be aware of technical levels as part of a global trading plan.

Trading the technical: Base your market perspective on graphical models, trend lines, support and resistance levels, and momentum studies. Technical traders usually identify a trading opportunity in their charts, but they must always be aware of key events because they are the catalyst for many technical breaks.

Trading Events and Data: Base your positions on the results of expected events, such as a rate decision from the central bank or a G7 meeting or individual data reports. Event / data traders usually open positions well in advance and close them when the result is known.

Short-term, high-frequency day trading

Short-term currency trading is different from short-term trading in most other markets. Short-Term trading of stocks or commodities usually means holding a position for one day for at least several days. However, due to liquidity and low spreads of supply and supply in currencies, prices fluctuate constantly in small increments. Constant and fluid currency price action allows speculators to trade on a very short-term basis and only want to capture a few pips in each transaction.

Short-term forex trading usually involves maintaining a position for a few seconds or minutes and rarely more than an hour. But the time factor is not the defining quality of short-term currency trading. Instead, pip fluctuations are important. Traders who follow a short-term trading style seek to profit by opening and closing positions multiple times after winning only a few pips, often as little as 1 or 2 pips.

When it comes to discipline, stockbrokers must be absolutely cruel when they make profits and losses. If you only wish to make a few pips in each trade, you can not lose much more than a few pips in each trade.

Working on the market requires an intuitive understanding of the market. (Some practitioners call this rhythm trading.) Money changers do not care much about fundamentals. If you ask a scalper for his opinion on a specific currency pair, she is likely to respond to the "Looks Bid " or "Looks Offered " lines (that is, she feels buying or underlying sales in the market - but at that time). If you ask again a few minutes later, she can answer in the opposite direction.

Successful stockbrokers have absolutely no loyalty to one position. They would not care less if the currency pair went up or down. They are strictly focused on next glitches. Their position works for them, or they come out faster than you can blink. All they need is volatility and liquidity.

Here are some other essential guidelines to bear in mind when following a short-term trading strategy:

Only trade in the most liquid currency pairs such as EUR / USD, USD / JPY, EUR / GBP, EUR / JPY, and EUR /

CHF. **The most liquid pairs have the narrowest trading spreads and the least sudden price jumps.**

Different strokes for different folks

Once you have thought about the time and resources you can devote to currency trading and the approach you favor (technical, fundamental, or mixed), the next step is to choose the trading style that you want. Is best. Corresponds to these choices

In the following segments, we detail the three main trading styles and what they really mean for individual traders. Our goal here is not to advocate a particular trading style because styles often overlap, and you can adopt different styles for different business opportunities or different market conditions. Instead, our goal is to give an idea of the different approaches used by forex traders so that you can fully understand the basis of each style.

Making time for market analysis

Calculating the amount of data and news that flows through the forex market on a daily basis can be really overwhelming. So, how can a trader track all the data and news?

The key is to develop an effective daily market analysis routine. Through the internet and online currency brokers, independent traders can access a variety of information.

The bottom line is the large pool of news and information that reflects the macroeconomic and political fortunes of countries whose currencies are traded. In most cases, when you hear someone talking about the fundamentals of a currency, it refers to economic fundamentals.

We do not know many currency traders who do not follow any form of technical analysis in their trading. Even stereotypical marketers who practice anything are probably aware of the technical price levels identified by others. If you are a trader active in other financial markets, you have probably done a technical analysis or at least heard about it.

Technical analysis can provide insights into the path of major price changes, allowing traders to predict the scope and direction of future price changes more accurately. More importantly, technical analysis is the key to building a well-defined trading strategy. For instance, your fundamental analysis, data expectations, or simple instinct may lead you to conclude that the USD / JPY is down. But where exactly do you fail? Where do you make profits, and where do you reduce your losses? You can use technical analysis to refine the points of entry and exit of trading and decide if and where to add positions or reduce them.

Sometimes foreign markets seem to be more due to fundamental factors such as current economic data and comments from a central bank official. At that time, the foundations provide the catalysts for breaks and technical reversals. At other times, technical growth seems to be leading the charge - an interruption in trend line support can trigger long-term stop-loss sales and incorporate system models that are sold according to the interruption of support. Later economic reports may be against directional theft, but the data must be damaged - the media is finished, and the market is selling.

The market approach with a mix of fundamental and technical analysis increases your chances of detecting business opportunities and managing your business more effectively. You will also be better prepared to deal with markets that react alternatively to key technical developments or a combination of both.

Real-world and lifestyle considerations

Before you begin to identify the style and approach to trading that's right for you, think carefully about the resources you have to support your trading. As in most of the efforts of life , when it comes to trading on the financial market, there are two main features that people seem never enough: time and money. Deciding how much each one you can spend on currency trading helps to establish how you are pursuing your trading goals.

If you are a full-time trader, you have a lot of time to devote to market analysis and trading in the market. But as currencies are traded nonstop, you must always know which trading session you are trading in and the daily peaks and valleys of activity and liquidity. (See Chapter 1 for specific session details.) Just because the market is always open does not mean it's always a perfect time to trade.

If you own a full-time job, your boss may not like to take the time to follow charts or economic data reports while you are at work. This implies that you will have to use your free time to do your market research. Be realistic in thinking about how much time you can regularly spend, taking into account family obligations and other personal circumstances.

As far as money is concerned, we can not emphasize enough that commercial capital must be venture capital, and you should never risk money that you can not afford to lose. The default definition of venture capital is money that, if lost, will not significantly affect your standard of living. Needless to say, borrowed money is not ventured capital - you should never use borrowed money for speculative transactions.

By determining the amount of venture capital you have for trading, you'll have a better idea of the size of the account you can trade and the size of the position you can manage. Most online trading platforms usually offer generous leverage ratios that let you control a larger position with less margin required. But it's not because they offer high leverage that you need to use it fully.

CHAPTER 14:

FOREX STRUCTURE AND PARTICIPANTS.

The FX structure

Unlike stocks and futures, Forex is a decentralized marketplace. Meaning, Forex does not have to go through a central exchange like New York Stock Exchange (NYSE), or London Stock Exchange, or any other exchange, there are 21 of them, by the way. Instead, the Fx market has multiple exchange centers around the world: Frankfurt, New York, Tokyo, Hong Kong, Sydney...

Even though it is decentralized, there is still structure and hierarchy to the forex marketplace. The top-tier includes the largest banks in the world: Citibank, JPMorgan, Union Bank of Switzerland (UBS), Deutsche Bank, Goldman Sachs and more. This is known as the Interbank. The Interbank market is basically a network between the largest banks. This network functions through the EBS (electronic broking services) and Reuters spot matching systems.

Basically, the EBS and the Reuters platforms are competitors that have effectively split the market share between them. Most of the Institutional firms use either one or both. The difference between these two, the liquidity that they provide on certain currency pairs and the price they charge for their services. One thing is obvious, they are quite expensive for the retail participants.

The Interbank market manages Forex order transactions for themselves (Banks) and their customers (Institutional and Commercial participants). Both of these applications efficiently aggregate the order books of the interlinked banks, displaying the countless bids/offers and, most importantly, the amounts that each is inclined to transact at.

Essentially, the Interbank creates market exchange rates based on the supply and demand of a particular currency. This creates the currency exchange market as we know it. Furthermore, the big banks are responsible for the bid/ask spreads, speculators must pay up when placing their trades.

Note:

On the Interbank level, each financial institution records its transactions with the other participants in the market and keeps these records private. That is why the information is not available to the public eye. Even though sometimes you will find volume data in the spot Forex market, it's never the true volume of the whole FX marketplace, but merely a fractional volume of the above mentioned banks, or a specific brokerage house.

As I've mentioned above, when banks deal with one another, they are aware of the different rates being offered. The prices the banks actually obtain rely on the credit relationship between the two Institutions; the better the credit standing between the two banks, the better are the rates. The approach is comparable to a consumer trying to receive financing from a credit company.

Even though, the Interbank market is not regulated by the authorities, the self-regulation of the participants turns out to be highly effective as it allows only the best and most qualified financial Institutions to trade in this arena.

Note:

Due to the fact that the forex market is decentralized, the price provided for a particular trading instrument will differ depending on the brokerage. Given, that there is no intermediary (Exchange) in the FX market, dealing costs are substantially lower and order execution is pretty fast.

Just as with everything else, both the Interbank marketplace and the centralized exchanges have their benefits and disadvantages. Nevertheless, it is for this simple reason, the decentralized aspect of the Forex market, that makes it so effortlessly accessible to the everyday retail speculator.

The foreign currency exchange is a decentralized marketplace with a global trading network where the largest banks deal and create the prices of a security directly amongst themselves.

This enables proper market performance by supplying plenty of liquidity as well as effective order processing. The Interbank market is exclusively available to large banking Institutions, well-established financial Institutions and large private accredited investors. This is primarily done to eliminate any counterparty risk, and to cut down the competition. By limiting availability to the Interbank market the big banks continue to uphold the lion's share of the Fx turnover.

The Participants

Let's take a closer look at the participants and learn more about our competition.

Governments and Central Banks

The Federal Reserve (FED), the European Central Bank (ECB), the Bank of England (BOE), all are examples of the government bodies and the central banks which deal in the foreign exchange market. Governments have to interact with other countries for International trade payments, operational purposes, and exchange their reserves.

There are good reasons why the central banks are at the top of the ladder in the FX marketplace. I call them "the guardians of the currencies." Let's face it, they are the entities with the ability to actually create money. They also can influence the market expectation verbally, by means of speeches, highlighting their views on the Economy and/or with direct interventions.

They have the power and the means to intervene with the

forex market when they believe that the price of their currency is either too high or too low. The banks often initiate a massive selling or buying campaigns to realign exchange rates. Central banks also adjust interest rates to control inflationary pressure which can affect currency valuation.

Major Banks, "The Big-10"

At the top of the food chain we have, the foreign exchange dealers. These are the dealer-banks, which conduct foreign exchange business for their clients and for themselves. The major banks include: Citigroup, JP Morgan, UBS, Deutsche Bank, Bank of America, Barclays Capital, Goldman Sachs, HSBC, RBS, and Morgan Stanley.

These financial behemoths are responsible for approximately two-thirds of the daily forex volume. Above mentioned banks deal with each other on behalf of their clients, or for themselves, and yes, they are actively involved in speculative transactions. They provide much- needed liquidity to the marketplace, so large transactions can be facilitated and properly executed.

The dealer-banks that form the Interbank space, in essence, are the market-makers of the forex industry. They supply the liquidity, manage the volume, and set the prices for the rest of the market to feed off.

Hedge Funds, Institutional Speculators, Commercials Players

On the next level of the forex ladder we have the market that exists for financial and non-financial participants. This may include: hedge funds, mutual & pension funds, smaller banks, businesses and large private speculators.

Commercial companies that deal Internationally must also go through the foreign exchange market, to buy goods, raw materials, or services from another country. These companies can also affect the currency exchange rates, when merger and acquisitions (MA) takes place; two large cross border companies merging, or when one company is acquiring another. In such cases, companies go to commercial banks to perform these types of transactions.

Hedge funds and large Institutional speculators are among the most well-funded currency traders group. They have deep pockets and can easily influence currency trends, because of the massive size of their trades. Hedge funds invest on behalf of individuals, businesses, private and commercial organizations, sometimes even countries. Because of this, they are regarded as the most experienced market competitors and use a number of different methods, such as: discretionary trading, semi-algorithmic trading, as well as, completely automated high frequency trading, also known as HFT's.

Retail Market Makers (STPs & ECNs)

Essentially, the retail forex brokers are the middleman party between buyers and sellers, which means they facilitate the financial transactions between the end user and their liquidity provider, in this case, the market-maker bank.

The retail market-makers (brokerage houses) provide additional liquidity to the forex market by repackaging large contract sizes from the wholesalers (Dealer Bank, Commercial Bank) to small contract sizes. This, in return, allows the retail speculator, as a group, to enter into the FX marketplace and compete with the "Big-Boys."

Brokers will normally have an agreement with one, or a number of liquidity providers through which they get the quotes, hedge positions on their books, and mitigate any exposure they might have. A liquidity provider might be any of the above mentioned major banks, or even another retail broker depending on their agreement and their need.

Most retail forex brokers use either, electronic communications network (ECN) or straight through processing (STP) programs. ECNs and STPs are the dealing platforms that execute customers buy/sell orders at the current market prices. The market making banks dictate the prices that are quoted by these platforms. Most ECN/STP brokers usually charge a commission plus a spread to open trades. However, because of the nature of their business model, they offer tighter spreads that of a non ECN/STP brokers.

Note:

Retail market-makers, as well as, smaller hedge funds do not have strong credit relationships with the Interbank market. Hence, this group has to conduct their business with commercial banks.

Retail Traders

At the bottom of the Forex structure, there are the retail traders, traders like me and you. Gladly for us, because of the Internet revolution, and what came after, the electronic trading, retail traders can now be involved with the forex market. We have been given access to participate in the largest market and compete with hedge funds, banks, commercial corporations.

Note:

The Forex was primarily designed for the use by bankers and large financial Institutions. However, in the late 1990s, with the growing popularity of the Internet, and the growth of online forex houses, the Foreign Exchange market was finally opened to the public.

It should be clear by now, that the variety of forex market participants buy and sell currencies for very different reasons. Central banks influence the FX markets through their monetary policies, interest rate adjustments, and currency interventions. Their job is to keep the currency and the economy in check. Corporations involved in currency trading are there to hedge their risk that comes from International business operations. Their job is to hedge their business risk and for this reason they are the most knowledgeable group amongst the players. Hedge funds, mutual and pension funds along with individual investors are considered to be profit-driven speculative traders. Their job is to make good returns for themselves and for their clients.

The foreign exchange marketplace is a well-designed, well-oiled machine that is kept in balance through hawkish supervision by the central banks. It is a sophisticated, two-tiered financial ecosystem that accommodates array of participants: commercial banks and non-bank exchange dealers, corporate funds, firms conducting commercials and investment transactions, small accredited investors, as well as, retail foreign exchange brokers.

CHAPTER 15: BUDGETING FOR PROFIT, RISK MANAGEMENT, LEVERAGE, AND TIME FRAME

This chapter focuses on how to budget for profit when trading forex and expounds on how you can manage risk and use leverage to your advantage. The chapter also addresses how the timeframe affects operations in forex. The risk management strategies in this chapter especially, are essential for your success as a trader.

Budgeting for profit

Budgeting for profit means that you have to understand how the forex market works. You will have to understand risk and other basic concepts and how to manage your account. In this chapter is an explanation of how to budget for profit, how to manage risk, an in-depth look at leverage and time frame as it relates to forex.

If you want to make profits when forex trading, there are a few tips you can use. For instance, ensure that you start small. This advice applies mainly to those who are new to forex trading; you can only be successful at trading millions when you have learned how to handle a few dollars as you can be successful in trading dollars when you have learned how to trade pennies. If you are lucky enough to buy many small stocks, there is a probability that they could tremendously increase in value, earning you profits. Luckily, there are traders today who can allow you to open an account with just a few dollars. If you constantly use the account, over time, your profits will begin to grow, and you will begin to experience success.

Additionally, if you want to succeed, you should be a regular investor. This does not mean you have to put in huge chunks of money for trading each time. It simply means that you could add manageable amounts to your investment every week — for instance, $10 or $20 per week. Being a regular investor not only refines your craft but also grows a sizeable account when the profits are compounded over time. When you invest small amounts, you will not feel the pinch, but the rewards will be great regardless.

Another tip when budgeting for profit is to be patient. As has been highlighted above, starting small is a good move. However, many people get frustrated because of the slow process. To enhance your tolerance, trade small, but do not view these small amounts as dollars. Instead, view them as percentages. If you get a profit of, let us say $1 when you have a $10 dollar account, then you have made a 10% profit.

On the other hand, if you lose a dollar, then you have lost 10%. You will then have learned a valuable lesson about forex trading at a low cost of just a dollar. Also, when you trade in bits, you learn to deal with the hurdles associated with learning how to trade forex.

Risk management

Risk management involves reducing the size of potential losses while getting the most benefit out of a single trade. Risk management is highly-debated as a topic in forex trading and, yet, it remains important as an aspect of trading because of the volatile nature of the forex market. To understand risk management in detail, read on.

One of the fundamental rules of managing risk when trading forex is to ensure that you only risk what you can afford to lose. Interestingly, many traders make the mistake of investing more than they can afford to lose, especially when they are learning the trade. As a forex trader, however, you can avoid some of the fundamental mistakes made by traders and become an outstanding trader yourself. You should know when to cut your losses. Cutting of losses can be done in two ways. The first is when you impose a mental stop and decide that the right thing to do would be to limit the drawdown, you can take on a trade. Another way through which you can control losses is by using a trading platform that has technology that allows you to lock in stops when your losses reach a particular level.

To control risks, you can also use the correct lot sizes. When accounts are advertised by brokers, they make it seem like a good idea to open an account with, let us say, $300 and use leverage to enhance mini-lot trades. They make it look like this technique will help double your money in just a single trade. This kind of thinking can sometimes deviate so far from the reality. When starting as a new trader, it is important to start small so that you have many options for managing the trade.

You should also be able to track your overall exposure. Reducing lot size is a good step to take. However, other steps, such as opening many lots with currency pairs, could have serious implications. For instance, when you go long on USD/CHF and short on EUR/USD, you are exposed twice to the realities of the dollar movement. Should the dollar tumble, you will suffer double losses which can be a painful eventuality. If, however, you keep your exposure limited, you have better chances at reducing risk and increasing your chances at success in the future.

Trading with a plan is also essential. This is because when you have a plan, you can easily avoid emotional responses, which are a natural part of trading forex. Having a trading plan will help you know what steps to take from the beginning to the end of your trading session before you open a position. An additional pro of trading with a plan is that it will keep you from speculations and possible overtrading as a result of there being an open position. Understand that in forex, you have to have strong will power. Your trading plan is not going to work magically. You must have a plan and follow it to the latter for this risk management strategy to be effective.

Another risk management strategy that you can employ in your trading is to understand the nature of the currency pairs you have decided to trade. Understand the events scheduled to take place in the day and even week ahead and how the data looks. Look at your trade plan's time horizon and consider liquidity conditions. Have a clear view of what the market has priced in and out because anticipating market events can alert you of the possible disruptive circumstances even if it is not a complete indicator of how you can win a trade. By understanding that risk varies across currency pairs, based on different factors such as liquidity, data sensitivity, and volatility, you will be better placed at understanding the analytical tools and strategies that are best for you.

Also, you can trade with an edge. This means that you do not have to be in the market all the time despite the fact that the currency market operates round the clock. Block the noise and do not let it pull you in. You can do this, for instance, by picking a spot and timing yourself. Also, look for setups in which there is a clear risk/reward scenario to avoid an unnecessary headache. Being an opportunist in the real world can be a problem, but that does not mean this strategy cannot work in the digital world of forex trading. You can take your time looking at the coming trade opportunities and use these chances instead of getting caught up in the market moves of a single moment.

Look forward to future opportunities because there will be more opportunities and it pays to be ready.

Sometimes in life, it is good to take a step back from situations because it provides an individual with moments of clarity. This is why it is advisable to take a step back from forex trading as a whole sometimes. Yes, this means that you need to take time off the markets completely for a while and no, you will not miss out on important trades. On the contrary, when you take this break, you may find that it was much needed and that you are more objective when you trade and you have a clearer perspective that does not allow you to emotionally invest in a market position. Also, you can use this downtime to develop other skills, such as your understanding of fundamental analysis and to prepare yourself for fresh trading opportunities.

It is also important that as a trader, you take your profits regularly. When you take your profits, you are, in essence, reducing your exposure to risks in the market. You may find that your trade plan has an aggressive profit target, but imagine what would happen if events do not play in your favor. It is, therefore, a better idea to protect what you have already worked for instead.

Another piece of advice that is usually mostly off the books is that you should regularly take money out of your trading account, especially if you make profits. This is a tactic that can be referred to as taking money off the table. If you keep your profits in your margin account, you are likely to be subject to future trading decisions and are susceptible to unknown risks. Taking money out of your account keeps you in a position where you can trade in comfortable sizes. As you trade, remember that trading is not purely a game of profits, you can as well use the profits you make to do other things. You can invest the profits into another venture once you withdraw them.

Additionally, you should ensure accuracy by double-checking. By now, you must have understood that currency trading takes place in a fairly fast-paced environment. It is even faster, thanks to electronic trading. There is, therefore, a risk in human error when inputting orders and trades, and this may have serious implications for you as a trader. For instance, what would be the benefit of putting in place a stop-loss order if it not entered for the right amount of currency? As a result, it would pay to make it a part of your routine to double-check your order and trade entries to avoid unnecessary mistakes that may prove costly to your forex trading venture. Ideally, it would be good to double-check figures immediately you input them and just before submission. Mistakes happen, but this does not mean you let minor errors become the source of your downfall.

Leverage

By now, you must have an idea of what leverage is and what it can do for you in forex trading. In this section, however, we discuss leverage in detail.

In forex, leverage can be described as the ratio of the trader's funds that you are allowed to use to the size of the broker's available funds. In essence, leverage is whatever capital you borrow to increase your returns potentially. In reality, the leverage size usually exceeds invested capital to a large extent. Leverage is not fixed in all companies and may largely depend on the trading conditions provided by the forex brokers. Using leverage can sometimes be a risky affair because just like a double-edged sword, it may work to your favor or not. Below, we highlight how leverage works and how it can affect your bottom-line.

How leverage works

When you take leverage, it essentially means that you have borrowed from a broker. To calculate the margin-based average, you should divide your total transaction value by the amount of margin required.

The formula is thus:

Margin-Based Leverage = Total Value of Transaction / Margin Required

If therefore, you are required to top up 2% of the transaction's total value as margin, and you intend to trade a standard lot of USD/CHF equivalent to $200,000, the required margin would be 4,000 dollars. The margin-based leverage, in this case, would be 200,000/4,000, which equates to 50:1.

Interestingly, margin-based leverage does not affect risk. Whether a trader is required to top up a percentage of the transaction, therefore, does not influence the profits and losses they make. An investor always has the chance to attribute more than the required margin when trading. Real leverages rather than margin-based leverages have a stronger influence on profit and loss.

Calculating the real average would require you to divide the total face value of open positions by the capital you have for trading. As such:

Real Leverage = Total Value of Transaction / Total Trading Capital

For instance, let us say you have $20,000 in your our account and the position you open is worth $200,000 (one lot). Your leverage will be 200,000/20,000. If you traded two lots with the same amount in your account, then the leverage on your account would be 400,000/20,000, which is 20 times.

The margin-based leverage is, therefore, equal to the real leverage you can use to trade. Most traders, however, do not make use of their entire accounts as margin, and this is why their real and margin-based leverages tend to differ. It is generally advised that you do not use all your available margin. You should only use your leverage if you clearly have an advantage on your side.

You should first establish the extent of risk in terms of pips numbers so that you determine the potential capital loss you are likely to incur. The general rule states that the loss should be less than 3% of your capital, if you leverage a position and the potential loss comes to approximately 30% of the capital, then you should reduce your leverage by an equal 30%. As an experienced trader, you may deviate from the standard 3%.

You may also calculate the margin level that you should use, to determine the level of risk a trade poses. Let us say you have $

10,000 in your account and you decide that you are trading ten mini USD/JPY lots. A move in one pip in a mini account is around a dollar, but when trading minis, the amount rises to approximately $10 each. If you trade 100 minis, then a pip move will be worth approximately $100. If therefore, you take a stop-loss of 30 pips, you have a representation of a potential $30 in a mini lot and $3,000 for 100 mini lots. With $10,000, you should leverage 30 mini lots at most, even when you can possibly trade more.

CHAPTER 16:

FOREX MONEY MANAGEMENT

In this chapter, we will take a closer look at the importance of money management in FOREX trading. It goes without saying that becoming a savvy money manager will help you get the most out of your investments. In particular, your ability to make the most out of a small investment will make, or break, your profits and gains.

As such, you need to become proficient at money management if you truly wish to be successful at FOREX trading. The underlying factor that will make you a successful money manager in FOREX trading is the ability to keep your emotions in check.

Whenever I talk to folks about trading be it stocks, FOREX or any other type of asset, I always make a point about the importance of keeping emotions in check. You cannot expect to be successful if you let your emotions get the better of you. Whether greed or fear, your emotions can play tricks on your mind.

Perhaps the most important emotion to keep in check is greed. The reason for this is that are you become more proficient in FOREX trading; you will find that you could make more money than you had originally anticipated. The leads to a feeling of having left money on the table. In reality, there is no such thing. It is virtually impossible to ascertain with a high degree of precision as to the total amount of money you can expect to make in every deal.

Of course, you can run your numbers and come up with fairly accurate investments. However, FOREX has so many moving parts that the various variables in the air make it virtually impossible to nail down how much money you are going to make on a deal. In fact, you can end up making more than you anticipated and certainly less than.

Consequently, greed can bury itself in your mind and make you think that you can always make more money if you make a bigger bet. After all, you need money to make money, right? This is a flawed assumption as FOREX markets can turn on a dime. When this happens, the profit that you had anticipated can quickly get zapped and turn into a potential loss. The more you risk, the more you lose.

It is as simple as that.

That is why you need to learn the basics of the game and then understand the money management rules that govern FOREX traders. Once you have gotten a firm grasp of these rules, you can begin to really make headway. If you do not adhere to a specific system, then your assessment of trades will be all over the place. This will lead to flawed assumptions and even greater risk.

Consider this table when you make a FOREX trade:

Amount of money lost

Amount needed to recover lost balance

10%	50%	90%
11%	100%	1000%
25%	75%	
33%	400%	

As you can see, the more you lose, the more you need to recover in order to get back to your initial position.

So, if you lose 10% of your initial balance, you will need 11% to regain your original position. That doesn't sound too bad. But as you up at ante, the amount of money you need to make in order to regain your position grows exponentially.

This is not a simple game of doubling down. You can't expect to go all-in, lose, and then go double or nothing. If you do so, you will end up getting wiped out.

If you see me using a poker analogy, you are right. FOREX, without a proper game plan, is nothing more than a poker match. You have the option to make money and you have the same chance to lose everything. Any poker player will tell you that going all-in is one of the biggest risks you can ever make in your life.

So, my advice to you is to play conservatively. It is best to "leave money on the table", as it were, rather than going all-in and being wiped out by a miscalculation.

The importance of money management rules in FOREX

Now, there aren't any set of rules which you must follow, that is, there is not a magic system. Rather, there are a series of rules that are more like best practices. These are tried and true practices that experienced traders have learned from past mistakes and successes. These practices are not meant to be taken as dogma. Instead, they are meant to be seen by investors as a means of finding a balance between risk and sound money management practices.

As you gain experience in the FOREX markets, you will find that there is a clear reason why those before you devised these rules. In fact, most of these best practices came about because someone got wiped out at some point. So, the learning experience led them to come up with a rule that encapsulates the negative experiences that past investors went through.

In addition, being a rogue trader can be a lot of fun. It can bring a lot of excitement to your life and it can make FOREX trading go from being a speculative task to becoming an extreme sport. However, I can assure you that you won't last very long. At some point, you will get knocked out of the game.

Consequently, the need for clear rules in your investment plan is essential so that you can ensure that you will meet your goals and targets. Therefore, this is your starting point.

Determine the goals and targets you wish to achieve as a part of your investment strategy.

Are you looking to make some extra income?

That's fine.

Are you looking to make a decent living?

That's fine, too.

Are you looking to become rich?

Sure, that is a possibility as well.

Whatever you choose to pursue is alright. The only thing that you need to keep in mind is that whatever you choose to pursue must be dealt with in such a manner that your expectations are realistic. If your expectations are unrealistic, be it through unreasonable earnings or an unrealistic timeframe, then you will only become disappointed and you will be opening the door to greed.

As such, the first exercise I would like you to do is to write down your ultimate goal. Whatever it is. That will be your final destination. That will give you a target to shoot at. Of course, you can change your mind along the way, but it is important that you have a target in mind. Otherwise, you will just be taking shots in the dark hoping to hit anything and not what you really want to hit.

The golden rule of money management

Whenever you hear the term "golden rule" it means that said rule is very important.

In FOREX trading, there is one very important rule, a golden rule, which will help you navigate the waters.

But before we actually get into the golden rule (I'm building suspense, here), I should warn you that this is a very conservative rule. The reason for such a conservative rule is that FOREX can wipe you out, completely.

You see, when you trade stocks, you can actually hold on to them even if their value drops. As long as the company is profitable and they are paying out a dividend, you can actually get something out of it.

With FOREX, there is no such luck. If you get stuck with a bad trade, then you will have a depreciated asset that you may very well never recover. Think of all those folks who were holding Turkish Lira when its value plummeted. You can safely assume that they scrambled to dump their holdings.

The problem with trying to dump their position once the Lira was plummeting is that no one, in their right mind, would be looking to buy Lira. If anything, they would be waiting for the bottom to drop out completely before taking a position in Lira. So, the folks who had US Dollars or Euros stood to clean up once the dust settled. The folks that were holding Lira were basically willing to take anything they could get in order to cut their losses.

189

Now, compound this problem with an investor going all-in. Can you see how they could have been completely wiped out? The Turkish Lira lost approximately half of its value in a span of about three weeks.

Three weeks.

That's how fast currencies can get hammered by markets. As such, you don't want to be the one stuck with the check at the end of the party. You want to make sure you leave before things get out of hand.

Based on the previous example, the golden rule is:

Do not bet more than 2% of your investable assets on a single deal. And, do not bet more than 5% of your total assets on all of your deals combined.

That is very conservative. But it is not a question of risk aversion or being a scaredy-cat. It is about common sense.

If you lose 10% of your position, then you need to make 11% profit in your next deal just to break even. If you believe that making 11% back on a deal is tough, you would only be halfway right. Making 11% on a single deal is virtually impossible. That would imply having a currency lose 11% of its value in a single deal. Economically, that is a highly unlikely phenomenon.

Now, you might say, "I'm not banking on one currency tanking, I'm banking on another gaining in value". Alright, so, gaining

11% in one shot is next to impossible.

Do you see where I am going with this?

You cannot expect to make that much money in a single deal. However, you can expect to make 2% to 3% in a single deal, if you're lucky. Nevertheless, losing 2% (in the event that you are completely wiped out in that particular deal) is not going to bankrupt you. Then, making that 2% is not an insurmountable task. If anything, you can just as well make it back after a couple of successful deal.

Noe, there is one addendum that I like to personally make to the golden rule: please avoid doubling down on your bets. This will only open the door to further risk.

Let's consider an example.

You placed a trade for $100. This represented 2% of your investable assets. Now, let's also assume you got hammered and lost the $100. This means that you would need to make those $100 back.

Assuming a 2% return on the next deal, you would need to invest $5,000 in order to make a $100 profit off a 2% return.

Do you see how a $100 bet turns into a $5,000 gamble?

For the sake of arguments, let's say that you decided to double down and get out of the hole in one shot. So, you go double or noting and put the $5,000 in. And... you lose. You could be out five grand on pure speculation.

So, in a sense, it is better to lose $100 than to risk $5,000.

This is why the golden rule is golden. It is not the silver rule (well, it could have been platinum) nor is it the basic rule… or any other designation. If there is a single rule that you stick to, this should be the one.

But for the sake of learning, I would encourage you to go all-in on a practice account. You will quickly see how your money can quickly swirl around the drain.

Using stops in FOREX trading

"Stops" is short for "stop-loss" orders. These types of orders are also used in stock trading. They consist in setting a point in which the system automatically triggers a sell order so that unlimited loss is prevented.

This is part of the automation that you can utilize in your trading platform. However, don't get too overconfident that the system has got your back.

How so?

Remember my analogy about falling asleep at the wheel? When you are on autopilot, it is really easy to just put open positions out of your mind. So, if the deal goes south, the system automatically closes your position and you limit your losses. But the worst part of that is that you didn't actually learn much. You didn't really understand why the deal went south.

Why did you decide to fly manually?

That's just risky because your reactions as a human are infinitely slower than that of a machine. The machine will immediately trigger the sell order when the stop-loss point is triggered. Therefore, automation will help you reduce your reaction times to virtually zero. However, your attention to detail will enable you to avoid making the same mistake again.

Hence, automating your trades through the use of stops will enable you to make the most of the tools at your disposal.

Types of stops

There are four different types of stop. They are all used in different situations. You can make use of one, or all of them if you feel that is warranted.

Equity stop. This is when you set your stop-loss point as based on a specific percentage of your account. For example, you can configure the system to automatically sell everything off at whatever price when your equity falls to 90%. This would correspond to the 10% loss rule. However, a more responsible stop-loss point based on equity would be about 2% to 5%. This will allow you to cut your losses well before you are taken to the cleaners.

Chart stop. This is the most common type of stop as it is based on prices and/or resistance levels. For instance, you have a give exchange rate, so you set up your stop based on an exchange rate. Also, you might set it to a specific price point in which you may encounter a resistance level as identified by your analysis of the trends in that currency pair. Consequently, the system will sell off one position in particular, or all of them at once.

Volatility stop. This stop takes into account the range in price for the given currency pair. So, you might find that there is considerable fluctuation in the trading range. This is something that makes you uneasy, so you want to make sure you are covered if that range of such fluctuations exceed your tolerance level. The fluctuation is measure over a period of time which can range from a few minutes to several days.

Time stop. This type of stop is based on a given period of time. So, the system will sell off your position at a specific point in time. For instance, the selloff may occur at the end of the trading day, after several days, weeks, or even months. If you are day trading FOREX, you want to set up these stops at the end of the time you have allotted for trading. The last thing you want to do is call it a day with open positions. While the system will trigger its stops in case anything happens, remember that leaving open positions unattended is highly discouraged.

Let's look at an example of how a stop can be considered in a real-life example.

First of all, let's assume the following data:

A total investment account of $10,000 (total investable assets)

The golden rule set at 2% (total risk)

Maximum amount per trade is $200 (10,000 * 0.02 = 200).

Based on this, we are assuming a potential loss of $200 in the worst-case scenario.

Now, before entering a trade, you need to keep an eye out for the trend in your desired currency pair. You need to look at the highs and the lows. This will give you a trading range that you can comfortably determine. So, if you are banking on an upward trend, you want to get in when the price is at the low end.

At this point, you have seen the price come down to its low, so it's time to get in.

Now, the risk you are taking in your position is determined by a measurement called a "pip". This stands for a point in percentage. So, 100 pips make up 1%, otherwise known as a basis point. In essence, a pip equals 1/100th of 1%. Thus, it is a really small measure of the overall price of a transaction.

So, let's assume a pip level of 50, that 50/100 of 1%. This will be the figure that will trigger a chart stop. As a good rule of thumb, you should always incorporate a chart stop when you use any other type of stop. That way, you can ensure that you won't get wiped out completely.

Consequently, you can determine the actual dollar value of your chart stop. Take the total you are investing in a single deal and multiply that by the pip. In this case, 200/50 = 4. This is $4. Therefore, the maximum amount of risk you are willing to take in this deal is $4. Anything above that, even $4.01 will trigger the stop.

In this example, your position of $200 (the actual amount of currency you purchase will be determined by the exchange rate), will be protected, if you will, by a stop of $4. This entails that you can only lose a maximum of $4 on the deal before the system takes care of your position.

Thus, using stops can certainly help protect you and your assets. Bear in mind that regaining a small loss is far easier than making one huge bet and then having to dig your way out of an enormous hole. So, as I mentioned before, if there is one rule that you are going to follow, this should be it.

As you gain more experience in FOREX trading, you will be able to anticipate some of the toughest movements as a result of volatility. This will enable you to figure out when you need to get in, and what the best point for you to get out would be. So please take the time to become familiar with the use of stops. They can save you from disaster.

CONCLUSION

Forex as the largest and most liquid market in the world attracts a lot of new traders who expect to make a fortune, achieve financial freedom and become their own bosses. Unfortunately, very few traders see this come true in their trading careers. Most go bankrupt in a matter of a few months. Is it because the market is only for highly talented or those who have connections? No, everyone can be successful. Anyone who puts enough effort, time and learns from his trading mistakes can become a full time Forex trader.

This eBook has introduced you to basic principles of currency market, taught you about most famous trading strategies and chart patterns that can help you to be successful. It also explained you a few more key elements such as risk management and broker selection that you will need in order to survive in the market. Finally, we dealt with some key rules that every trader should have and keep to with discipline. Those rules will help one to move from a beginner to an intermediate and with enough effort and experience even to advanced level.

You may not become a billionaire or millionaire trading currencies, but if you are persistent, hard learning and not willing to give up you will eventually see that you are able to survive in the market and prosper. Be a learner. Learn from your mistakes. Set new targets and go forward in your career as a trader. Good luck!

CPSIA information can be obtained
at www.ICGtesting.com
Printed in the USA
LVHW041025291020
669936LV00003B/367